WATER
"The Elixir of Life" is Endangered

About the Author

Dr K.P. Agrawal obtained his B.V.Sc. & A.H (1968) and M.V.Sc. (1972) degrees from Veterinary College, Mathura and Ph.D. from I.V.R.I. Izatnagar in 1980. He worked in different Capacities: Research Assistant, Sr. Research Assistant, Scientist, Sr. Scientist at I.V.R.I Izatnagar (1972-1982): Associate Research Scientist/Associate Professor/Research Scientist at Veterinary College, Gujarat Agricultural University, Gujarat (1982-1984) and Scientist-S3/Principal Scientist/Head of Division at Central Institute for Research on Goats, Makhdoom (1985-1999). He was selected as Director, Department of Biotechnology, Ministry of Science and Technology, New Delhi in 1990. In 1999, he joined as National Coordinator in World Bank Aided National Agricultural Technology Project (NATP). As follow up of NATP, he continued as National Coordinator of another World Bank Aided National Agricultural Innovation Project (NAIP). He is life member of 13 Scientific Societies and 4 social organizations. He is recipient of several awards/honours during his academic and research career. He has 350 publications to his credit of which 30 are books, chapters in books, monographs and bulletins. He has wide experience of research, teaching, extension, research management, policy planning and institutional building. He retired from the post of National Coordinator, National Agricultural Innovation Project (ICAR) in 2007. After retirement, he worked for two years as senior consultant in a world bank supported project, "Water Sector Restructuring Project" in Madhya Pradesh. Presently, he is associated as chairman/member of several committees/academic committees in ICAR, Universities and other organizations.

WATER
"The Elixir of Life" is Endangered

Dr. K.P. Agrawal
Former National Coordinator
National Agricultural Innovation Project
Indian Council of Agricultural Research, New Delhi

CONCEPT PUBLISHING COMPANY PVT. LTD.
NEW DELHI-110059

ISBN-13 : 978-81-8069-903-0

First Published 2012

Published and Printed by

Concept Publishing Company Pvt. Ltd.
A/15-16, Commercial Block, Mohan Garden
New Delhi-110059 (India)
T: 25351460, 25351794, *F*: 091-11-25357109
E: publishing@conceptpub.com, W: www.conceptpub.com
Editorial Office: H-13, Bali Nagar, New Delhi-110 015, India.

Cataloging in Publication Data--Courtesy: D.K. Agencies (P) Ltd. <docinfo@dkagencies.com>

Agrawal, K. P.
Water : "the elixir of life" is endangered / K.P. Agrawal.
p. cm.
Includes index.
ISBN 9788180699030

1. Water supply—India. 2. Water supply—Government policy—India. 3. Water resources development—India. 4. Water resources development—Government policy—India. I. Title.

DDC 363.610954 23

From Author's Desk

Water is the most precious natural resource and an universal asset. The whole world is fast heading towards a water crisis. India in spite of being one of the wettest countries in the world is becoming a nation of acute water scarcity. The water related issues confronting the world as a whole and India in particular have been discussed in this book.

The book covers a wide range of water related issues like water resources, availability, demand and supply status, reasons of water crisis and its impacts on ecology, food security, national economy and health, strategies and action plan for secured and safe water supply in future. The focus is on water related issues from a national perspective. Delhi being national capital of the country, a separate chapter on water has been included in the book. The fourteen chapters covering different aspects have been included in the book and are arranged to ensure a logical flow of the theme.

The author realized the importance of water in national economy particularly in agriculture sector during his working as national coordinator in World Bank Aided National Agricultural Technology Project and National Agricultural Innovation Project for more than 8 years. Magsaysay Award winner Rajendra Singh, Anna Hajare, Bindeshwar Pathak, Late Dr. Anil Agrawal and several others have been the source of inspiration to take up this work. Last but not the least, the memories of my childhood when my grandfather used to rebuke me on any of my act of water wastage. He used to often remind me for using water sparingly and wasting even a drop of water was curse. The book is an outcome of inspirations from my grandfather and several others subsequently. Inputs from different sources, *viz.*, books, magazines, newspapers, ancient literature, eminent scholars, social scientists and environmentalists who had vast experience of research, field and administration have added value to the book.

My grateful thanks to different organization, media, scientists, social and extension workers and developmental agencies working on water management and allied sectors in the country. Without their support, it would not have been completed. It is also a pleasure to acknowledge the help rendered by Mr Pankaj for typing the manuscript. Last but not the least, I express my heartfelt appreciation to my wife Mrs Shakuntala Agrawal, my daughter-in-law Mrs Parul Agarwal, my son Mr Jayesh Agarwal and my grandsons Atharv and Naman for their wholehearted support and encouragement in writing the book.

The book will be useful to researchers, planners, social activists, environmentalists, farmers, industrialists, domestic users and anyone who has concern about water and its importance.

New Delhi **Dr. K.P. Agrawal**

Contents

1
Introduction

Water is the greatest gift of nature. All religious scriptures around the World mentioned about the importance of water. In India, water offerings are made to Gods as a sacred ritual since time immemorial. Among various kinds of 'dana', 'the jal dana' is considered the best. A couplet recited by Rahim about importance of water is mentioned here: "Rahiman Paani Raakhiye, Bin Paani Sab Soon; Paani Gaye Na Ubare Moti, Manas, Choon". World is fast heading towards a water crisis. Its shortage is likely to be so acute that the next world war may be fought on sharing of water resources among various countries. Quarrels on water sharing within the country and community are common.

According to the UN estimates, the total amount of water on earth is about 1400 million cubic kilometer (m.cu.km.) which is enough to cover the earth with a layer of 3000 meters depth. The potable water constitutes 2.7 per cent of the total water of which about 75.2 per cent lies frozen in polar regions, 22.6 per cent as ground water and 2.2 per cent is available in lakes, rivers, atmosphere, moisture, soil and vegetation. Only 0.5 per cent of the water on the planet is available for human use. Globally, per capita availability which was 16,900 cubic meters in 1950 decreased to 6,800 cubic meters in 2000 and is expected to further decrease to 5,400 cubic meters by 2025.

The situation in India is disturbing because we have only 2.45 per cent of the world's landmass to support 16 per cent of the world's population. Of the available water, 74 per cent is shared for agriculture, 18 per cent for hydro-power and

8 per cent for households. Water available for domestic purposes is scarce according to international standards. Water availability in the country has come down from 6,500 cubic meters to 2,500 cubic meters per person per annum which will be further reduced to a stress level of 1,000 cubic meters per person per annum from 2020 onwards. With population growth and change in lifestyle, the annual demand is expected to increase at least two-fold by 2030 (demand 1,500 cubic km against projected availability of 744 cubic km).

The water demand in Delhi is about 1,000 MGD and supply is 670 MGD. Delhi gets raw water from Yamuna, Ganga, Bhakra Beas Management Board and ground water. The ground water which is the primary source of water for drinking and irrigation purposes is depleting fast and is unable to meet the demand. The quality is also deteriorating (with high levels of chlorides, sulfides and nitrates) and is not safe for use. According to CII report, Delhi's water table is falling almost 10 feet per annum and has dropped to 350 feet in most places as compared to 30-40 feet at the time of Independence. With a projected population of 25 million in 2025, Delhi would need an additional 1,200 MGD of water which is difficult to meet with existing resources. The water scarcity in newly coming up colonies is acute. The case of Dwarka, the biggest colony in Delhi is cited for reference. MCD supply which is less than an hour a day hardly fulfills 20-25 per cent of demand. The residents are mostly dependent on ground water which is also scarce and of sub-standard quality. With an acute shortage of water, the residents have to depend on DJB or private water tankers that charge about Rs. 1000 for a tanker load which is neither affordable nor sustainable in long-run.

The water is not only a sparse commodity but is dangerously polluted too. Its impact on health, production and economy is visible. The Delhi being the mirror of the country is facing serious problems in managing the water crisis. The issues and reasons for the present crisis are manifold. Growing population, increasing industrialization and urbanization coupled with poor management of water resources are main reasons of present water crisis. In spite of several schemes on rainwater harvesting, two-third of rainwater flows in the sea. Out of the total annual precipitation of about 4000 Billion Cubic Meters (BCM), the annual availability of water is about 1120 BCM in the country. Construction of *pucca* roads, flats, industrial establishments and government offices in most of the metropolitans has left very little open *kachcha* space through which surface water can percolate into the ground. In Delhi alone, such concrete expansion covering about 370 square kms of agricultural area has deprived of 89 MGD groundwater recharge through seepage if the city gets normal rainfall of 40 cm in the monsoon. Further, construction work in ridge area and in the Yamuna basin has adversely affected and would continue to affect groundwater recharge. The situations in Delhi are different. Of the total water produced in Delhi (730 MGD), 345 MGD (about 50%) is leaked through different sources like water treatment plants, through pipelines and theft directly from the pipelines. Over three lakh illegal booster pumps pull out water before it reaches the residents located at the end of network. 30 per cent of rainwater along with industrial and household effluents goes as waste in gutter, 60 per cent rainwater is drained in sea through river and hardly 10 per cent rainwater is harvested for domestic and other uses. Delhi Jal Board (DJB) supplies about 6 MGD water through tankers (both DJB's and private tankers). Black marketing by private tanker owners and unconcernness of DJB are main hurdles in ensuring water supply. Installation of GPS system in board's tankers also failed to check the pilferage. Unequal distribution like 30 litres per capita per day of water supply in some areas compared to 500 litres per capita per day in VIP areas (much above the national standard - 130 litres per person per day) is responsible for water crisis. Other reasons of diminishing water supply and deterioration in water quality are contamination of waterways and underground water by untreated sewage and waste water discharge. About 700 water bodies (ponds, lakes, baolis etc.) in Delhi because of their heavy silting, being used as garbage dumps and their encroachment have resulted in drastic reduction in storage capacity and ultimately poor recharge of groundwater. Opening of sewage drains in several water bodies have polluted both surface and groundwater. Delhi contributes 80 per cent of total Yamuna pollution. More than 50 per cent (384 MGD) of Delhi's total domestic sewage (710 MGD) discharged untreated in Yamuna is responsible for its pollution.

India which was one of the wettest countries in the world is becoming a nation of acute water scarcity. A case of Delhi is cited here. Billions of rupees spent on water related projects did not provide any respite to Delhites. A number of projects: (1) Installation of Sonia Vihar water treatment plant to supply 140 MGD water to South and East Delhi, (2) Cementing of 'kachcha' Munak canal to save 80 MGD water for water treatment plants at Bawana, Okhla and Dwarka, (3) Construction of Renuka dam in Himachal Pradesh to provide 275 MGD water to Delhi, (4) Kishan dam and Lakhwar Vyasi dam in Uttaranchal to provide 275 MGD and 135 MGD water respectively, (5) Installation of 4 water recycling plants for utilizing 40 MGD water which otherwise is discarded as waste water generated during water treatment operations, (6) Construction of 50 underground reservoirs to augment water supply and (7) DJB's Interceptor Sewage Technology Project to clean Yamuna initiated by Delhi Government, DDA, DJB and CPCB to meet the city's water needs did not provide respite to water crisis. Many projects are yet to take-off.

All strategies to overcome the water crisis have failed. We simply talk of water conservation techniques, judicious use of water and recycling techniques but we never practice. According to an estimate, we use more than three times the quantity of water than is actually required. The country may face an acute water scarcity if water related issues are not addressed in a focussed manner. All the efforts should aim for sustainable development and quality improvement of water resources. Rainwater harvesting, groundwater recharge, judicious use of water, avoiding water waste and recycling of waste water are important steps to mitigate the water crisis. There is a need for participatory approach (both individual and community based) with financial assistance from government, NGOs and other institutions. Available resources should be captured and used efficiently for maximum benefits.

The book covers overall water scenario of the country in respect of water resources, availability and supply status, water pollution, water crisis and water woes, its impact on ecology, food security, national economy and health, water management and conservation strategies and an implementable action plan in project mode for secured and safe water supply in future.

2
Water Resources, Availability, Demand and Supply

Water Resources

Ancient literature enjoins merit to a person who constructs wells, dams and other structures. Even invaders from abroad could understand the wealth of water. Ghiyasuddin Tughlaq who ruled India for 3 decades (1220 to 1250) encouraged digging of canals. The Vedas and ancient Indian scriptures made references to wells, canals, tanks and dams as potential water resources. India has immense reservoirs of water in the form of Himalayas in the North, the Arabian Sea in the West, the Indian Ocean in the South and the Bay of Bengal in the East. Our concern in this chapter is mainly with fresh water which is available as surface water (reservoirs, lakes, rivers etc.) and groundwater.

Surface Water Resources

Surface water resources of the country are rivers and canals, tanks and ponds, beels and lakes. The total length of rivers and canals is 183.6 thousand km of which about 17 per cent is occupied by rivers and canals of Uttar Pradesh. Other states following Uttar Pradesh are Jammu and Kashmir and Madhya Pradesh. Other than rivers and canals, the water bodies cover an area of about 7 m. ha. of which tanks and ponds have maximum area (2.9 m. ha.), followed by reservoirs (2.1 m. ha.) and beels and lakes (2.0 m. ha.). The area under tanks and ponds in Andhra Pradesh, Karnataka and Tamil Nadu, West Bengal, Rajasthan and Uttar Pradesh (in descending order) account for 62 per cent of total area under tanks and ponds in the country. States like Andhra Pradesh, Gujarat, Karnataka, Madhya Pradesh, Maharashtra, Orissa, Rajasthan and Uttar Pradesh account for large portion of area under reservoirs. India is a country of many rivers. Twelve rivers are classified as major rivers whose catchment area is 252.8 million hectare (m. ha.). Of the major rivers, the Ganga-Brahmaputra-Meghana system is the biggest with 43 per cent (about 110 m. ha) of the catchment area of all the major rivers in the country. The catchment area of medium rivers is about 25 m. ha. Unfortunately, many rivers in our country are poor vestiges of the past due to their long neglect. The Ganga, the Yamuna, the Krishna and the Godhavari are in pathetic state.

Many water bodies like tanks, ponds and lakes are disappearing as sources of water in the country. An example of Delhi, the national capital of the country is cited. As per survey in 2000 by Tapas, a NGO, there were 794 bodies in Delhi. Of which many are at different level of encroachment and others are left as shallow pits. Hardly any attention is being given to revive and/or improve these water bodies. Rather the water bodies are being targeted as potential real estate and builders' lobby in connivance with bureaucrats and politicians who are allowing them to choke to death.

Groundwater

The groundwater contributes about 50 per cent of water for irrigation and 70-80 per cent for domestic use in rural areas and 50 per cent in urban and industrial areas. 432 bcm groundwater can be annually replenished in the country. Out of which, about 71 bcm is used for domestic, industrial and other uses and remaining 361 bcm for irrigation. Use of groundwater beyond this will have an adverse effect on groundwater quantity and quality. Few examples of adverse manifestations of groundwater over extraction are arsenic poisoning in West Bengal; increased salinity in Gujarat, Haryana, Punjab,

Karnataka, Rajasthan and Tamil Nadu and high fluoride levels in peninsular India and western part of the country. About 2 crore tube wells/bore wells in the country are extracting groundwater day and night in the country to fulfill 70 to 80 per cent water requirement for irrigation and domestic use.

Precipitation

India's average annual precipitation is about 1,170 mm covering a land area of 3.28 million sq. km. Thus, the volume of annual precipitation comes to 3,840 cubic km. Of total precipitation, about 17.5 per cent water evaporates immediately from the soil, 37.5 per cent flood out into the sea and 20 per cent for various hydrological purposes, leaving only 25 per cent (about 960 cu. km.) water available for different purposes by human beings. About 75 per cent loss is because of uneven spatial and temporal distribution of rainfall in our country. Easy availability of groundwater, simple and successful tube well technology and subsidy on diesel, electricity and even on tube wells made the task of ground-water extraction easier and less expensive. Erratic water supply and poor maintenance of canals have compelled people to go for digging tube wells both for domestic and irrigation purposes. The situation becomes more grave with increase in population and change in lifestyle. About 30 per cent of the country's population are mining much more groundwater than is recharged every year.

Water Availability

The total amount of water on earth is about 1400 million cubic kilometer (m.cu.km.) which is enough to cover the earth with a layer of 3000 meters depth. Of the total water, 97.5 per cent is sea/salt water and 2.5 per cent is fresh water. Of fresh water about 75.2 per cent lies frozen in polar regions, 22.6 per cent as groundwater and 2.2 per cent is available in lakes, rivers, ponds, atmospheric moisture, soil and vegetation. If all the ice of Antarctica is melted, the level of the oceans would rise by

200 feet that would flood one-fourth of the land. About 2,000,000 cubic miles of fresh water is stored within 1½ miles of the earth surface. In spite of such a huge quantity of water, only 0.5 per cent of the water on the planet is available for human use. Globally, per capita availability which was 16,900 cubic meters in 1950 decreased to 6,800 cubic meters in 2000 and is expected to further decrease to 5,400 cubic meters by 2025.

The situation in India is disturbing because we have only 2.45 per cent of the world's landmass to support 16 per cent of the world's population. The average annual water availability through different resources are: total precipitation – 4000 BCM, water availability – 1969 BCM, utilizable water – 1123 BCM (surface water – 690 BCM and groundwater – 433 BCM). According to UN's World Water Development Report of 2005, India ranked 133 among 180 countries in terms of water availability and at the bottom among 122 nations in terms of quality. Although, annual water availability in the country remains more or less fixed, the per capita water availability is reducing exponentially due to increasing population, industrialization and urbanization. As a result, the per capita water availability in India came down from 5300 m^3 in 1955 to 2200 m^3 in the early nineties against the world's average of 7400 m^3. The per capita water availability in some of the east flowing river basin of Tamil Nadu is as low as 380 m^3, while it is as high as 18,400 m^3 in the Brahmaputra basin. The per capita availability by the year 2025 and 2050 is projected as 1465 m^3 and 1235 m^3 respectively. Whereas with population growth and change in lifestyle, the annual demand is expected to increase at least two-fold by 2030. Reduction in per capita water availability, deterioration in quality of water and over-exploitation of groundwater resources are challenges before the country to face. The water supply in Delhi is woefully inadequate. The groundwater which is the primary source of water for drinking and irrigation purposes is depleting fast and is unable to meet the demand. Delhi's Jal Board claim of having 250 litres per capita per day (LCPD) of water which is quite a decent amount is beyond understandable. The water supply in newly coming up colonies is acute. The case of Dwarka, the biggest colony of Delhi is cited here. Water supply is not even an hour daily. Dwarka residents had only one thing in mind 'the water', particularly in summers. Bore wells have dried in most of the societies. Getting water through tankers is not only expensive but also difficult during water scarcity period. On an average, a Dwarka resident gets 50 litres of water a day – just enough to flush five times. The residents who can afford, depend on bottle water not only for drinking but also for taking bath and kitchen work, others suffer.

Demand–Supply Gap

Widening of demand–supply gap is global phenomenon. As income rises, food habits change in favour of more nutritious and diversified diets, the consumption of water increases. Shift from cereals to meat requires 10 times more water for 1 kg of meat. It is estimated that over 25 per cent increase in demand is due to dietary changes besides population growth. That will influence future agricultural water requirement by double in the next 50 years. According to a study by Water Resources Group, the water demand will increase almost two-fold (1498 bcm) to existing 700 bcm by 2030 if immediate steps are not taken. 70 to 80 per cent of total demand is for agriculture. 85 per cent of rural India and 55 per cent of urban India's drinking water needs are met from groundwater. Household use of water in rural and urban India is about 150 and 250 litres per person per day respectively. If the amount of water used in industrial and agricultural processes is added to this, each person's consumption increases to at least 10 fold per day.

The water demand in Delhi is about 1,000 MGD and supply is 670 MGD. The ground water which is the primary source of water for drinking and irrigation purposes is depleting fast and is unable to meet the demand. According to CII report, Delhi's water table is falling almost 10 feet per annum and has dropped to 350 feet in most places as compared to 30-40 feet at the time of independence. With a projected population of 25 million in 2025, Delhi would need an additional 1,200 MGD water which is difficult to meet with existing resources. Water scarcity in newly coming up colonies is acute. The case of Dwarka, the biggest colony in Delhi is cited for reference. MCD supply which is less than an hour a day hardly fulfills 20-25 per cent of demand. The residents are mostly dependent on groundwater which is also scarce. 3 million gallons (i.e. 25 to 30 per cent of requirement) of water supply through Delhi Jal Board of which 30-40 per cent is leaked, tapped before it reaches to the end users, makes the situation worst. The unauthorized colonies located around the sub-city also share the limited water supply to Dwarka. On an average, a resident of Dwarka gets less than 50 litres of water per day. That too is erratic and quality is not good. The proposed water treatment plant with 50 million gallon capacity has remained on the drawing board for about a decade. Even Munak Canal which was supposed to address the water problem of Dwarka is politicized. Is establishing Dwarka without making any concrete plan for ensuring water supply to the area and leaving the residents thirsty for about a decade not a criminal act? Water supply to Dwarka needs augmentation as top priority.

3
Rivers are Thirsty and Dirty

The rivers are lifeline and seat of civilization throughout the world since time immemorial. The rivers also have a greater significance in the history of Indian culture. Our bonding with the rivers is old. Mahatma Gandhi set off for the "Dandi March" from the banks of Sabarmati River in 1930. India is a land of many rivers: 14 big rivers, 55 medium rivers and hundreds of small rivers that cover an area of about 329 million hectares. The total river length is approximately 45,000 kilometers catering needs of 80 per cent of the country's population. Millions of people particularly rural and agriculture oriented population in the country depend on rivers for their livelihoods and sustenance.

River Pollution

The rivers once considered the spiritual lifeline and source of sustenance are no more than the filthy drains in India. They are fast losing their ability to assimilate, regenerate and revive. Rivers like Ganga, Yamuna and Sabarmati are among top polluted rivers. The other rivers like Damodar in Bengal, Chalia in Calicut, Hoogli in Kolkata, Son in Bihar, Godawari in Andhra Pradesh, Kuan in Chennai, Kullu in Mumbai are equally polluted. Even groundwater in a range of 20 km of river basin is affected by polluted river. The Ganga and Brahmaputra that support close to 25 per cent of India's agricultural production and are known for unique biodiversity are also facing a big human onslaught. Water extraction, dam construction and pollution are killing Indian rivers. The major sources of pollutants are waste water from urban areas, dumping of garbage along the river side, discharge of chemical and industrial waste water, including idols during Dussehra, Durga Puja and Ganesh Chaturthi, dumping of carcasses (dead animals), half and unburnt human remains, flow of pesticides and insecticides from farmland. The level of pollution in few rivers is very high. The Gomati River receives approximately 400 million litres of sewage daily through 26 large and medium canals in and around Lucknow. The river has high level of cadmium, chromium, lead, zinc and cobalt. Persistent high contaminants from river system to ground aquifers has made the groundwater unfit for consumption. The Kali river in Karnataka has been found to contain high level (12 mg/litre) of mercury due to discharge of affluent from paper mills. The pollution level in two important rivers Ganga and Yamuna, has been covered separately.

Effects of River Pollution on Health and Ecology

Rivers contain thousands of species of fish and aquatic flora, provide water for agriculture and domestic use. Most immediate effect of pollution in rivers is on aquatic life and ecology. Heavy metals like lead, mercury, arsenic, nickel, cadmium and chromium from industrial effluents and idols immersed in the rivers are unhealthy and are life threatening to aquatic life. Mercury is highly toxic to life. Every fish in India swims in water with a thousand times more than optimal level of mercury. Fish eaters have been found to contain higher level of mercury in their blood. High level of fecal coliform bacteria in sewage is responsible for disease epidemics like cholera, tuberculosis, jaundice, typhoid etc. It is not only river pollution but slow or stagnant river flow is also a big hurdle for ensuring clean and continuous flow of rivers. The hydel projects on rivers are main constraints in maintaining the minimum flow. Shrinking of river width and change in their course due to habitation and construction activities at the river basin is apparent. The width of Yamuna in its 22 km course in

Delhi has reduced to half km from 3.5 km. Daryaganj in Delhi was named as Daryaganj as it was located at the bank of river Yamuna which is now 2-2.5 km away. The river Ganga which was originated from Gangotri and terminates in Bay of Bengal now originates about 17 km north of Gangotri. Several rivers world over have disappeared or left to drains now.

Strategies to Revive Rivers

In the past, several projects have been sanctioned for harnessing and reviving the rivers. Two decades old National River Conservation Programme in spite of spending more than Rs. 5,000 crore did not improve the health of the critically polluted rivers. An ambitious National River Project launched in 2008 to ensure proper conservation of rivers for improving irrigation and power production potential is yet to take off. An amount of Rs. 817 crore on Ganga Action Plan and Rs. 1,306 crore on Yamuna Action Plan has been spent with no visible improvement. Sewage treatment plants established in different cities are working much below their capacity. Strategies should be clear with a focussed and time bound action plan. There is no use to launch the projects once the river is polluted and has reached to a point of no return. It has to be an on-going process. The aim should be to develop time bound action plan and strategies with holistic approach to address the problem.

Unless river pollution is considered a national problem, steps taken by government including interventions by honourable court will not work. The local communities who depend on rivers must be involved. Children can be a driving force to create awareness.

The projects related to cleaning rivers are mostly funded by the Central Government but water being a state subject, monitoring of any such project becomes difficult. As a result, the ambitious projects to clean major rivers like the Ganga and Yamuna are unable to achieve the desired results. The work is also affected by multiplicity of authorities overseeing such projects. Declaring some of the most polluted rivers of the country as "National Rivers" will facilitate the Centre's direct intervention to clean up such rivers. The "National Rivers" concept mooted in 2006, is yet to take off.

The idol immersion in rivers and chemicals used therein cause heavy pollution of rivers. Our efforts should be to make sure that no element in the idol that has an adverse effect on health and ecology is used in the idol making. The people who are engaged in making the idols should be educated to use safe colours. Vegetable colours being costly, a policy should be framed to provide such colours at subsidized rates to idol makers.

The Water Resource Ministry should issue guidelines to all Ministries and State Governments to use water conservation devices.

Fee should be imposed on users for providing water for commercial use. Even water used for domestic purpose should be taxed to reduce wastage.

Dam construction, as a last resort should be done only when other water management schemes are not feasible.

Afforestation and public awareness programme to protect the rivers should be initiated.

YAMUNA, THE LIFELINE OF THE COUNTRY IS IN DANGER

The Yamuna after originating from Yamunotri in Uttarakashi district of Uttarakhand flows 1,370 km through many towns and cities downstream and merges with Ganga in Prayag. The stretch between Delhi (Wazirabad) and Etawah is highly polluted due to effluents from Faridabad, Gurgaon, Karnal, Panipat, Sonepat, Yamunanagar, Ghaziabad, Muzaffarnagar, Noida, Saharanpur, Mathura, Vrindaban, Agra and Etawah. Its water is full of carcinogens, effluents, sewage and domestic waste and is not only unfit for drink but also unfit for bath and cleaning cloths. The situation of both Yamuna flow and water quality is alarming. Yamuna basin is falling at the annual rate of 0.15 m per year. The flow in summer is reduced to 5 cubic meters per second which is much below the required flow of at least 58 cubic meters per second needed to dilute wastes drained in the river.

Delhi's history is intrinsically linked to Yamuna. It enters in Delhi from Wazirabad Barrage and passes through Okhala Barrage. In its 22 km course in Delhi, the river receives huge amount of sewage, domestic waste and industrial effluents that results in a sluggish sewage drain with stinking filth, plastic and toxic chemicals. Delhi which constitutes only 2 per cent of the catchment area of Yamuna, is responsible for about 80 per cent of its pollution load. The Yamuna from Wazirabad to Okhla has become one of the most threatened riverine ecosystems of the world. The water which flows in Yamuna is not even of C-category. The pathetic state of Yamuna mainly covering its 22 km course in Delhi is given below.

Yamuna Pollution

The river loses its colour and character during its 22 km course in Delhi. Biochemical Oxygen Demand (BOD) level has gone up (35 milligram/litre) as against 3 milligram/litre and Dissolved Oxygen Level (DOL) has come down to an alarming zero as against minimum of 5mg/litre. Total coliform are 2.4 crore/100 ml as against 5,000/100 ml, the prescribed norms. No aquatic life can survive under these conditions. Water is not fit even for irrigation particularly for vegetable crops which are eaten raw. River is no more a stinky drain in spite of spending more than Rs. 1,400 crore on cleaning up 22 km of river passing through Delhi.

The pollution in the river is mainly due to untreated sewage, dumping of garbage, industrial effluents, domestic waste, animal carcasses, *puja* material, encroachments and construction of unauthorized colonies on the river banks and along the drains. According to the report of Central Pollution Control Board, Delhi alone spills about 4,300 million litres (MLD) of sewage into 22 km stretch of the river everyday as against treatment capacity of 2,330 million litres per day. 22 drains keep belching the city's sewage into the river. The major drains are: Burari drain, Najafgarh drain, Civil Mill drain, Power House drain, Dr. Sen's Nursing Home drain, Barapulla drain and Shahadra drain.

There are more than 60,000 slum dwellings inhabiting about 3.5 lakh people on the river banks and along the drains. These slums contribute significantly to the Yamuna's pollution by discharging all types of wastes directly into the river. Other than that, majority of people living in the unauthorized colonies and Jhuggi-Jhopari cluster dump solid waste into the open that ultimately block the drains. Use of flyash on riverbed also pollutes the water.

During festive season like Dussehra, Durga Puja and Diwali, the immersion of *puja* material and its ill effects on the river water have been highlighted time and again for past few years. According to an estimate, it is roughly 36 tonnes of paints, 18 tonnes of oil and polish and equal amount of flowers, leaves, coconut husks, straw and bamboo.

Massive construction work in recent years on river banks and throwing of solid wastes have added to the problem of pollution and scanty river flow. The width of the river has narrowed down from 3.5 km to less than half kilometer. The shortage of sewage treatment, insufficient sanitation facilities, lack of awareness and civic sense towards sanitation add to the problem.

Steps Taken So Far Have Not Yielded Concrete Results

The work on cleaning Yamuna river is going on for many years. A string of elaborate action plans have been announced by different agencies. More than Rs. 1,500 crore spent by different agencies have not yielded concrete results. Rather Yamuna has become more polluted over the years.

1. A three-stage plan to clean Yamuna was developed by DDA about three decades back. The plan included: (1) installing a sewage treatment plant on each drain before falling in the river, (2) constructing a canal parallel to the river, connecting all sewer drains in it and diverting the water after cleaning to Haryana for irrigation purpose and (3) channelizing the river and concretizing the river bank after an uniform width and

removing silt to allow rainwater to retain in Delhi. The plan was not executed.

2. The Yamuna Action Plan which had to improve the quality of water along the 22 km stretch of Delhi and adjoining areas of Haryana and UP did not make any improvement in spite of spending Rs. 1,500 crore under Yamuna Action Plan I & II. Out of 30 sewage treatment plants, hardly 10 are fully functional. Only 15 per cent of 33,000 MLD sewage is treated, remaining 85 per cent goes in the river.
3. An ambitious Rs. 2,000 crore project was announced in 2007 by the DJB to restore the river on the same lines as the Thames. An agreement was signed between Delhi Jal Board (DJB) and Engineers India Ltd (EIL) to lay interceptor lines along three major drains – the Najafgarh drain, Supplementary drain and the Shahadra drain to ensure that untreated sewage water did not flow into the river. With this interception approach, it was expected that by 2010, the capital could have a clean Yamuna river. A decision was taken to set up 18 Sewage Treatment Plants (STPs) at the mouth of each drain joining the river. More interestingly, the Delhi Jal Board had conceded in an RTI reply that the treated water is not even fit for bathing. Therefore, the main purpose of interceptor Sewer Project seems to be defeated. Spending such a huge amount without turning treated water even fit for bathing is simply a waste.
4. Very recently, DJB initiated another plan to save the river. Six NGOs were roped in. A public outreach programme, "Aao Jamuna Mein Jaan Daalein" under the Yamuna Action Plan (YAP)-II, especially involving the children was initiated.
5. Noida Authority also initiated construction of 4 sewer treatment plants on Yamuna and Hindan bank to make Noida zero discharge city by 2015. The plan is to use water from water treatment plant for irrigation and construction work and silt after drying to be used as manure. The target was to make these treatment plants

functional before Commonwealth Games. The work plan is not yet ready.

6. The issue to clean Yamuna before Commonwealth Games was raised since early 2007. A huge amount under different projects has been spent. Yamuna is as filthy as before. Chief Minister of Delhi expressed her helplessness on Government failure of river cleaning with following statement. "Both Yamuna Action Plans had failed and Yamuna had reduced to a drain. Any fresh initiative would take at least 7 to 8 years to show results. All attempts for cleaning Yamuna before Commonwealth Games have been futile and Yamuna is as filthy as before."
7. Even court interventions to clean Yamuna have been futile. The Supreme Court as early as in 2000 directed Environment and Forest Ministry for fixing 2005 as the deadline to clean the Yamuna. The Court also directed the Ministry to file an affidavit detailing the steps, the authorities had taken to keep the river pollution free. Delhi High Court in 2008 appointed Yamuna Panel to assess the progress of projects related to Commonwealth Games. The panel strongly opposed construction of any concrete structure on the river bed. Nothing moved forward.
8. According to section 24 of the Water (Prevention of Pollution) Act, 1974, discharge of dirty water into the river was banned. The discharge continued to pour in with utter disregard to the Act. Unstable and frequent changes in plans with no focussed approach of DJB, Delhi Government and other agencies are reasons of failure. Despite spending thousands of crores of rupees and Court's directives, nothing tangible has been achieved. There is complete violation of law including Court's directives.

Reasons of Failures

Agencies like CPCB, DJB, MCD, DDA and Delhi Government,

all accept that the river is highly polluted and the measures taken so far to clean the river have failed. The excuses given by these agencies for failure are: (1) sewage treatment is very expensive and costs Rs. 50 lakh to treat a million litres per day, (2) shortage of sewage treatment plants of which many remain non-functional, (3) more than 60,000 slums on Yamuna bank are difficult to be relocated due to non-availability of land and (4) lack of expertise available in the country. With such excuses, should we stop working for cleaning Yamuna and let Yamuna be a river of the past? Are we really serious to clean the river? If "Yes", what steps are we taking for not allowing further increase in slums and/or sewage flow in river or to reduce the cost of sewage treatment? What are half a dozen agencies doing if they cannot manage cleaning of Yamuna.

Involvement of half-a-dozen agencies are adversely affecting the progress of Yamuna projects. One agency puts blame on another. Absence of coordination between different agencies adds confusion. Each agency has its own agenda and priorities, e.g., for Department of Environment, priority is to afforest one kilometer wide area along the river's course, while DDA would like to develop parks and recreational areas which would require many concrete structures. Cleaning of Yamuna seems to be no body's baby. But when it comes to the fund allotment, everyone wants to stand first in queue.

Lack of sincerity on the part of authorities to rejuvenate the river is major factor for failure. Recommendations based on several studies are taken in a casual manner. Vote bank politics is a big hazard. Politicians are responsible to encourage mushrooming of slums in the capital. All encroachments on the river banks and on the bank of drains cannot be salvaged so long vote bank politics has a upper hand. There is lack of will and determination to address the problem. Most of the problems are our own creation.

Strategies and Action Plan to Rejuvenate Yamuna

The river is putrefied and almost dead from Wazirabad onwards. Reviving the river to its original stage is a difficult task. About 50 years ago, the Hudson river in New York was as bad as the Yamuna. But with sustained efforts and community participation, the river reversed back to its original state. Why that cannot be done with the Yamuna? The country has spent thousands of crores of rupees in cleaning Yamuna without any results. Cosmetic and piecemeal approach aiming short-term gains and quick returns will not work. Pollution abatement is not a one-time effort and demands sustained approach with increase in population and expansion of townships. The need is for holistic approach and a time bound action plan. A river is not simply a flow of water. It includes riverbeds, local ecology and the banks. All these points should be taken into consideration and future strategies should be developed in that direction.

The riverbed area in Delhi (from Wazirabad to Okhla) is 97 sq km. The whole of the riverbed area has coarse grain sand up to a depth of 40 meters which is key to the riverbed's water recharge. With massive concrete work, much of the riverbed has already been lost. Due to construction structures and coming up of numerous bridges, the flood plain has been narrowed down and the river has substantially lost its carrying capacity due to heavy silting. The present width of the river should be maintained at any cost. Better is to forget what we have lost. We should wake up now. No further construction and encroachment should be allowed. All unauthorized inhabitants on riverbed should be removed and inhabitated elsewhere. The government should work with partnership mode with private agencies.

Large-scale extraction of river water at the upstream of Delhi for drinking and irrigation purposes has led to a negligible flow in the river after Wazirabad. Measures should be taken for improving river flow. Entry of drainage waste into the river should be stopped. Regular dredging and desilting improve carrying capacity and river flow. About 50 per cent of water is wasted in Delhi due to leakage. It should be prevented. Walls should be constructed on both sides of the river to stop narrowing down of the river bed width. To keep flow of the river and for maintaining sufficient water, an agreement with neighbouring states should be developed. There should be ban on further extension of city inhabitation.

"Too many cooks spoil the broth" is applicable to the efforts of multiple agencies engaged in cleaning Yamuna. A single authority to override the problem of multiple agencies should be appointed. The authority must be empowered to issue directions to any department or agency and its decision should be binding on all the agencies. A Nodal Authority that works efficiently, keeps corruption at bay and coordinates well with other agencies should be constituted. It should be given authority so that the decision-making process becomes easy for smooth discharge of work. Agencies responsible for inordinate delay should be penalized. Private players should also be roped in for the project. Industries discharging effluents into the river should be penalized. Accountability and transparency should be maintained at all costs.

A blueprint to contain pollution in the city should be developed. Sewage (treated or untreated) should not be allowed to fall in the river. The treated sewage should be diverted through canal for agricultural work or put back into the ground. Putting back treated water into the ground would recharge the groundwater level. The approach would result in zero flow of sewage into the river. River cleaning programmes should be pursued diligently and finished in a time bound manner. Dense afforestation particularly trees like eucalyptus which have heavy rates of transpiration should be avoided.

Yamuna Yatra should be organized to spread awareness about pollution and saving of river. It should be a ritual. A day should be declared as 'Save River Day'. Different important rivers covering mainly the rivers passing through cities should be the main focus on this day. School children should be involved in creating awareness. Various competitions and rallies should be organized on Yamuna rejuvenation. Riverbanks should be beautified so that people come there and understand the importance of river. Public should be made aware during the festive season about the adverse effects of idol immersion and other *puja* material. Traditional clay and water soluble and no-toxic natural dyes should be used in making the idols.

Last but not the least, strong political will, commitment, serious and concerted efforts and focussed approach are mantras for the success of the programme.

GANGA IS UNDER THREAT

Ganga, the India's most culturally, spiritually and economically important river has a special place in our hearts and minds. It has long been a symbol of communal and national harmony. Numerous poems have been written on The Ganga. Saqib Kanpuri in his poem 'Ganga Isnan' has written innumerable qualities of Ganga water. People used to feel pride to live in India and narrate "Main Us Desh Ka Vaasee Hoon, Jis Desh Mein Ganga Behti Hai". That glory of Ganga is now under threat.

Ganga as Bhagirathi originates from Gaumukh at the edge of Gangotri Glacier and enters the plains at Haridwar. The total length of the river is 2,500 km of which 1,450 km flows in India. The Ganga flows in India in four states: Uttarakhand, Uttar Pradesh, Bihar and West Bengal. The Ganga basin (the area drained by river) has 26 per cent of India's land area covering 2,900 towns. More than 30 per cent of the country's population live in the Ganga basin, making it one of the world's most densely populated river basins and provides livelihoods to millions of people. The Gangetic Plain is considered one of the most fertile land in the country. In Bihar, farmers soak their seeds in Ganga water before sowing to ensure a good harvest. Ganga water is considered the purest and the most puissant purifier in the world. No germs can flourish in it. It is said that the glacier from which the Ganga originates rests on a mountain which has special minerals/micro-organisms (bacteriophase) that kill germs and keep the water drinkable even when stored for months/years.

Ganga Pollution and its Effect on Health and Ecology

Ganga is losing its purity and flow. The World Wild Fund

(WWF) in 2008 declared Ganga among the 10 most endangered rivers in the world. The river pollution is increasing fast because of discharge of untreated domestic and industrial effluents. The BOD in Ganga water in Kanpur had reached to 6.80 which is much higher than standard value (3 mg/litre). Several fold increase in coliform bacteria in Ganga water (2,40,000 per 100 ml) in kanpur has made Ganga water unfit for bathing and drinking.

Gangajal which is used as 'Achman' is source of several diseases. According to World Bank report, 9 to 12 per cent diseases in UP are due to Gangajal. A joint study by the Indian and Japanese doctors for over two years found that Indo-Gangetic Belt between Delhi and Patna had the second highest rate of gall bladder cancer occurrence in the world. The abnormally high rate is primarily due to pollution of the Ganga water and the soil around with heavy metals like lead, chromium and cadmium.

Ganga is one of the world's most rapidly shrinking rivers and is likely to shrink even faster in future. The waning of Ganga will reduce the supply of water for domestic and agricultural use and will have huge economic and ecological impacts in long-run. The river flow has become sluggish due to melting of glaciers, dam construction and growing habitat pressure. Melting of glaciers due to global warming will result in loss of ice mass and fall in rainfall over the years. Construction of a cascade of dams will turn the river into multiple stagnant pools. No doubt dams provide power supply but its long-term effects are manifold: (1) depriving rivers of the silt, a fertile soil, (2) resuction in microflora and microfauna, (3) increase in landslide and earthquake occurrence, (4) sluggish flow of water will provide suitable environment for mosquitoes to grow, (5) loss of land and displacement of people, (6) loss to the forest reserves and biodiversity, (7) disturbance in fragile Himalayan environment and (8) deterioration in quality of Ganga water.

Causes of Ganga Pollution

Ganga is one of the 10 major dying rivers in the world. The

Hooghly, the last 250 km stretch of the Ganga is on deathbed. About 27 million litre sewage and industrial effluents are poured in Ganga daily as it traverses its 2,500 km course. Cities/towns located along the Ganga river are main polluters. Religious rituals are equally responsible for polluting Ganga. Hundreds of dead bodies brought to Varanasi for last rites are flown even half burnt in the Ganga. Pollution starts at "Har ki Pauri" which literally means "Stairway to God" at Haridwar, "the Gate to God". Polythene bags, earthern lamps, flowers, garlands, coconuts and other *puja* material used at the time of *Aarti* in the evening are thrown in the river. Receding Gangotri glacier, the expansion of agriculture, deforestation in the catchments and rapid withdrawal of water have also contributed significantly to river pollution. Overexploitation of Ganga water for agriculture is another cause of pollution. The creation of dams on Ganga at Tehri has converted it into a cesspool of stagnant water.

The Schemes to Clean Ganga Have Failed

The Ganga remains one of the most polluted rivers in the world in spite of spending crores of rupees on different schemes since 1985. Union Government launched Ganga Action Plan in 1985 to reduce pollution level in the river. The plan involved the interception of *nullahs*, construction of sewage treatment plants, public toilets and electric crematoria along the banks of Ganga and monitoring of polluting industries belching effluents into the river. During 13 years of launch (1998) and sanction of rupees 500 crore to Uttar Pradesh, Bihar and West Bengal Governments, there was no respite in pollution. Rather pollution multiplied near important cities like Kanpur, Varanasi and Allahabad. Ganga became polluted to a level that Central Pollution Control Board declared its water unfit for drinking and other domestic use.

Ganga Action Plan is a bitter fact of Government failure. The money spent so far has gone in drains. Most of the sewage treatment plants built under Ganga Action Plan are not working satisfactorily. Other reasons for the failures are unconcernness, lack of interest and political will, poor planning and monitoring and frequent change in strategies. In fact, total machinery that includes bureaucracy, contractors, agents and politicians are responsible for present state of affairs. For politicians, the source of vote bank which is bread and butter for them is the top priority. Ganga, Yamuna and other rivers are never in their priorities. On failure, the concerned agencies come out with excuses like escalating population, expensive treatment plants, high operational expenses, global warming and other problems.

Ganga was declared National River in November, 2008. Prime Minister of the country in February, 2009 announced formation of National Ganga River Basin Authority (NGRBA) and asked the Ministry of Environment and Forest to develop the framework for the Authority for rejuvenating the river with a holistic approach rather than going for piecemeal efforts. NGRBA decided that no untreated sewage would be released into the river after 2020. An amount of Rs. 15,000 crore was approved for the work. The present capacity of sewage treatment plants (about 1,000 million litres per day) in the country would be enhanced by about 3,000 million litres per day. Social audit would be arranged to monitor the expenditure. The approach in the project would be catchment area treatment and river basin management rather than city based approach. The detailed action plan would be developed by December, 2010. Respective states were asked to contribute 30 per cent of the total budget and develop a detailed project report on requirement of sewage treatment plants for installing on the banks of Ganga and other supporting rivers. The independent experts of NGRBA in its first report submitted to Government in March, 2010 blamed Tehri dam and the Maneri Bhali I and II barrages mainly responsible for destroying the free flow character of Ganga. The people are sceptical about this project like the other projects which did not make any improvement in Ganga pollution and Ganga flow. The target date, December 2010 for developing action plan is over. There seems to be no progress till date.

Future Strategies and Action Plan

Ganga is a filthy drain. Its water is not fit even for bath and irrigation. If we do not wake up and allow Himalayan glaciers to melt, Ganga will be left to a seasonal drain. Declaring Ganga a national river and announcing a number of schemes to protect the river should not simply be a pre-election stunt. No improvement is expected with government machinery and bureaucracy alone. There is need for public-private participation and large scale campaign to create public awareness. There should be ban on establishing industries in Himalayan region. The country should go for massive plantation in the area. Keeping in view the operational costs and limitations of centralized sewage treatment, composting waste at the site or process it in other useful ways should be the approach.

The focus under Ganga River Basin Authority should be the river basin, pollution abatement, sustainable use of water and flood management. Various agencies working in different aspects of river conservation and pollution management should work with integrated approach. Detailed time bound action plan should be prepared after wide ranging consultancies. The current piecemeal efforts in selected cities must be replaced with holistic approach on issues related to its ecology, quantity and quality of water.

Under "Clean Ganga Mission", the concerned states should prepare detailed project reports on critically polluted hot spots and major towns located on the Ganga and major tributaries including a comprehensive river basin management plan. The total programme should be in a project mode that includes preparation of document for 10 years, time bound, state-wise and basin-wise action plan, clarity of action points, duration to achieve them, budget requirement, details of developmental and technical work, monitoring and evaluation framework, environmental and social framework, output, outcome and impact including post–project sustainability plan.

It is not only the money; more important is the commitment of Government and public. When Thames in London, Potamek in America and Rine in Europe which at one time were more polluted than Ganga, can be revived, why not ours. There is need for political will. It is time to wake up and save the great river and the great civilization.

4
Interlinking of Rivers

In spite of higher rainfall compared with other major continental areas, water is a scarce commodity in India. This is because of uneven spatial and temporal rainfall in the country. The river interlinking project was envisaged for joining rivers through reservoirs and canals to remove this natural imbalance. The plan was to divert water from water surplus area to water deficient area with an aim to alleviate flood and drought problems, to enhance hydropower production and availability of water for agriculture and domestic purposes.

As early as 1972, the then Irrigation Minister, Mr. K.L. Rao proposed to link Ganga and Kauvery with 2640 km canal. The issue was discussed at different levels without any concrete outcome in a span of 25 years. It was again in 1999, the issue to linking rivers was raised by NDA Government. A high level task force was constituted as per Supreme Court directives in 2002 to study the feasibility of linking country's drainage systems. River Link Pact (RLP) was conceived by NDA Government in 2003 with an aim to connect 30 rivers across India – 14 in Himalayan region and 16 in peninsular region with targets to irrigate 37 million hectares of land, generate 34,000 million kilowatts of electricity, control floods and prevent droughts.

First MoU signed on Ken-Betwa river link between Madhya Pradesh and Uttar Pradesh Governments in August, 2005 can be used as a litmus test before taking up a grandiose project of linking India's rivers. The issues related to sharing of water (1020 mcm) and cost (Rs. 8,300 crore), relocation and resettlement of about 8,550 people and submerge of about 8,650 hectares land including 6,400 hectares of forest area were not finalized in MoU. A few contentious issues like (1) drying of Ken river to a little stream in summer may further aggravate the situation and (2) building more dams in the upstream area of Ken which may render old dams, weirs and canals redundant were also not discussed in MoU. Other distressing issues which may arise on project implementation are: (1) Ken and Betwa flow through the same part of the country with similar topography and rainfall patterns. When one is in spate, so is the other. In dry season, both have little water, (2) Betwa joins Yamuna upstream from Ken. If it carries more water, the region between the two rivers will be flooded during the monsoon while areas downstream from Ken will have droughts during rest of the year. The project, therefore, will neither mitigate floods nor droughts, rather it will aggravate the situation through the link canal, (3) Displacement of people and huge project cost are additional disadvantages of the project, (4) Even experts have not been in unison about success of the project from the very beginning. Their opinions are contradictory. Unless such contentious issues are handled, resettlement and implementation plans are carefully drawn and the affected people are consulted, the project cannot succeed. Similar is the situation with other river linking projects. Any project without evaluating its social, economic and environmental implications may prove disastrous in long-run.

Experts' Views about River Linking Project

The views of the experts who favour river linking project are: (1) to reduce incidence of floods and droughts, (2) to enhance availability of water, (3) to enhance hydro-power generation and (4) to divert water from water surplus area to water deficient area and therefore saving huge amount of river water which is flowing into the sea. The group supporting interlinking project cites examples of China and Australia where vast dry area has been converted into green belt by interlinking few important rivers.

The views of the group who do not support the project are different. Rivers have their natural course. Interlinking the rivers diverse their course which is an artificial approach and may be hazardous in long-run. With construction of dams and canals, there will be displacement of people, uprooting of trees, disturbance in ecology and perishing of aquatic life. The project will lead to destruction of cultures, communities and ecosystems of the country. It will create rifts between States and regions. The group antagonistic to interlinking rivers even support the river flooding due to many reasons. Flooding is a constructive geographical process. It creates fertile plains by depositing nutrient rich sediments, recharge the groundwater into the farmland and sustains many riparian habitats. Low frequency and high magnitude floods add new cultivable farmlands. Soviet Union is an example of adverse effects of river linking. When Swolen and Snomelt rivers of Soviet Union were interlinked with Amu and Sair rivers of Mid Asia by 2,200 km canals, cotton production was reduced drastically. The plan to end flood problems in certain areas may not be successful because of limited lifting capacity (1,500 cubic meters) of water per second as compared to water flow per second in few rivers (normal volume of floods in the Ganga, Brahmaputra, Mahanadi and Godavari range between 30,000 and 60,000 cubic meters). During monsoon, when there is excess water in Brahmputra, the Ganga will also be in spate and even storage reservoirs will overflow, the very purpose of the project to control flood is bound to be defeated. The group even does not support the view that river linking would save huge amount of water which is flowing in the sea. Consequences due to less supply of water to the oceans are: (1) Marine life will be deprived of nutrients supply that may adversely affect marine productivity and (2) may affect the summer monsoon in Bay of Bengal.

There are other adverse effects of river interlinking project. Construction of a large number of huge dams and canals will have ecological and social consequences. Removal of suspended sediment load from the stream flow will leave irrigation water flowing down-stream of the dams nutrient depleted that ultimately affects crop production. Construction of thousands of kilometers of canals in the project area will entail a loss of large tracts of land to canals and reservoirs, national parks and sanctuaries and affecting the flora and fauna of the region. Huge canal networks of Punjab to augment irrigation for agriculture has proved disastrous. Over-exploitation of water resources has led to waterlogging and salinity and rendered millions of hectares of good land infertile.

River water and its use is state subject. Several rivers are passing through more than one state. Dispute on sharing of water will further increase with linking of rivers. Dispute between Karnataka and Tamil Nadu on water sharing from Kauvery is known to everybody. Even Supreme Court's directive to Karnataka to release Kauvery water to Tamil Nadu was flouted. It may lead to dispute between countries like Bangladesh, Nepal, Bhutan and China as many rivers pass through these countries.

The estimated project cost of Rs. 10 lakh crore may put a severe drain on government revenues and resources and shatter the nation's economy if results are not favourable. Several other projects of social and economic importance might have to be shelved or the country had to depend for such a huge funds on World Bank and other agencies and as security had to mortgage rivers, like the country once mortgaged roads and bridges against borrowed money. With such staggering cost and anticipated problems, the project may ultimately be a failure. Consumption of enormous amount of electricity for pumping water will be a great drain on our energy resources. The river linking project would also be against the two institutions constituted by the Government: Tiger Task Force to protect the tigers and Tribals Rights Group to recognize the rights of the tribals.

Summary

A river is an ecological system and one cannot think of connecting them like ordinary pipelines. Neither rivers can be compared with canals which are man-made. There is lot of biodiversity in it. It sustains the livelihood of all species living in and around it.

There are disputes on sharing of river water. States, districts, communities and families are fighting for water and are at the risk of division. The situation is chaotic. If we can not unite them, then uniting rivers passing across the states and districts will not be possible. Linking of rivers is complex and not cost-effective in long-run. Better is not to disturb the natural course of rivers.

We have already done lot of damage to the environment. Forest cover is reduced significantly resulting decline in rainfall. Natural process of water conservation has been dismantled. Then what do we expect by linking the rivers? Can we revive sanctity of river Yamuna which is merely a sewer drain by connecting with Brahmputra. First destroy, then revive has been the policy of most of the schemes in our country.

Linking of river is a gigantic scheme and will take decades to complete. Long-term schemes are rarely successful as per our past experience. The scheme will cause massive human displacement. The construction of dams and excavation of thousands of kilometers of canals will destroy habitation, displacement of people, loss of millions of hectares of agricultural land, uprooting of trees, disturbance in ecology and loss of aquatic life. Such a mammoth project which may jeopardize national economy cannot be justified.

There is enough water on earth to meet the needs provided we know how to use it efficiently. We waste more than 50 per cent of water available from different sources. Even if we ship the immense glaciers of Antarctica to India, there will never be enough water if we do not change our habit of using water. Under the present mindset of people who do not use it carefully, equitably and economically, the present water crisis is beyond solution.

Interlinking of rivers is not a good water management policy and alone it will not serve any purpose. Alternatively, country must concentrate to revive traditional approaches of water harvesting and conservation like watershed management, renovation, restoration and maintenance of existing tanks and reservoirs including rainwater harvesting. Other steps that provide relief to water crisis are judicious use of water, do not waste even a single drop of water, adopting principle of more crops per drop of water in agriculture, restriction on pollution of water reservoirs by restricting entry of industrial effluents and sewage in water resources, rainwater harvesting, forest development and water conservation with people's participation. Israel having more desert area than India is an glaring example of water conservation. Israeli model of water conservation is based on Indian traditional technology. Can't we revive that? Finally, the interlinking river project will be the biggest human, economic and ecological disaster of independent India.

5
Water Pollution

Besides availability of water, the quality of water is equally crucial for life sustenance. Availability of quality water at the right place and at the required time is uncertain. The problem of quality water availability is throughout India. More than 20 states suffer from salinity, iron, fluoride and arsenic contamination. In spite of 80 per cent of earth's surface covered by water, there is hardly any source which can provide pure water. Water in many parts of the country is unfit even for bathing and washing the cloths. None of the water taps provides pure water in our country. Even bottled water is not safe and may contain high levels of pesticides.

The problem of water pollution is more in urban localities. In many cities, percentage of people who do not have access to piped water is very high. The situation in Delhi is alarming. As per Central Pollution Control Board Report (CPCB), the toxic quotient in Delhi's water is five times higher than WHO standards. In Dwarka which is one of the upcoming colony in Delhi, the TDS of bore well water at few places is as high as 5000 mg per litre and hardness as high as 2000 mg per litre in contrast to safe drinking water specification of BIS (TDS below 500 mg/litre) and hardness not more than 7.5 mg/litre. Potable water will soon be a rare commodity. With pollution on the rise, the day is not far when water will be sold at a premium in many parts of the country

Sources of Water Pollution

Water is polluted from three main sources: industrial effluents, domestic sewage and run-off from agriculture related activities.

Industrial water pollution is due to inadequate measures adopted by the industries for disposal of their effluents. Inadequate disposal of sewage, urban waste and dumping of garbage contaminate surface and groundwater. Waste generated by cities, where 35 per cent of country's people live, pollute over 70 per cent of the water resources. About 40,000 m litres of sewage from cities flows into the streams, rivers and sea according to a report by CPCB (January, 2010). Country treats only 31 per cent of the sewage generated everyday. The large scale use of fertilizers and pesticides in agriculture is responsible for contaminating both surface and groundwater. Animal wastes are another source of persistent pollution in some areas. Religious and social practices also contribute significantly to water pollution. Heavy metals and organo-chlorines leached from municipal and industrial dump sites lead to serious health hazards. Besides inorganic and bacteriological contamination of the groundwater, seepage from the sewage system and overflowing of sewers are other sources of pollution. In big cities where treated piped water is supplied, the excessive use of bore wells, booster pumps and sewage lines running close to rusted and broken water pipes also cause water contamination. During rains, overflow of drains, sewers add to water contamination.

The groundwater, rivers and other water bodies like lakes, ponds and tanks are dangerously polluted. Industrial effluents and sewage generated from cities and towns account for the major pollution load. 75 per cent of the sewage flowing into the rivers is municipal waste and remaining 25 per cent industrial. The Yamuna with 200 million litres of untreated water effluents and sewage dumped everyday has become one of the most polluted rivers in the world. Its water has no dissolved oxygen to support aquatic life. The bio-chemical oxygen demand (BOD) content, one of the most important indicators of pollution is 30-40 times higher of the permissible level (3 mg/l). Several rivers (Ganga, Yamuna, Sabarmati, Satluj etc.) and water bodies contain an alarming level of bacterial contamination. Uncontrolled extraction without commensurate recharge and leaching of pollutants from pesticides and fertilizers into the aquifers has also resulted in pollution of groundwater supplies. Industrial effluents and municipal solid wastes in addition to leachates from agriculture have emerged as the leading causes of pollution of groundwater.

Types of Water Pollutants

Water pollutants are categorized as microbial, chemical, oxygen depleting and nutrients. Microbial pollutants include pathogenic micro-organisms like bacteria, virus, protozoa. Their main source of origin are sewage. Chemicals like heavy metals and solvents from industrial effluents and pesticides, insecticides and herbicides from run-off of agricultural practices are most common water pollutants. Many chemical pollutants like detergents and oils are equally toxic. Many wastes are biodegradable in nature and can cause the serious problem of oxygen depletion i.e. lowering of Dissolved Oxygen (DO) level sometimes to zero that leads to suffocation for fish and other aqua life. Excessive use of nitrogenous and phosphate fertilizers in agriculture ultimately results in high nitrate and cadmium level in run off and contaminate the surface water. These chemicals can readily leach into groundwater. The elements like phosphorus and nitrogen available in water can cause nuisance growth of aquatic weeds and algae and can cause problems like choking of drains.

Water supply to more than two lakh habitations in the country contains dangerous level of heavy metals like arsenic, fluorides, nitrates, cadmium, lead, iron etc. Drinking water in one-third of India's 608 districts have high fluoride contents and one-fourth have problem of salinity and nitrate contents. Excessive use of fertilizers, besides sewage and animal wastes, has shot up nitrate levels in groundwater. The admissible nitrate concentration in water is 45 mg/litre. The high arsenic content in groundwater in some areas of Bihar has disastrous effects on health. The average arsenic content in the groundwater in several districts of Bengal and Bihar is 500 Parts Per Billion (PPB), reaching to as high as 1800 PPB in a village of

Bhojpur district in Bihar whereas World Health Organization (WHO) considered 50 PPB safe for human consumption. Many people left the village after more than 18 babies born blind during three months in 2004. Overexploitation of groundwater is considered the reason for increase in the fluoride and arsenic level in drinking water resources.

Water Quality Control Measures

More than a billion people world over lack clean water. Almost half the developing world's people are sick due to unsafe water and poor sanitation. Sustainable development starts with people's health and dignity. The situation is worst in our country. Lack of water quality standards and their poor implementation is responsible for the present water pollution menace in our country. With poor sewage management, agricultural run-off, discharge of untreated industrial effluents, large habitations on river banks and cultural and religious practices of people, any improvement in water quality is a stupendous task. Poor policies, mismanagement, lack of political will and rampant corruption in the system add to the problem. The agencies like Central Pollution Control Board, Central Groundwater Board do not have clear action plan, time bound programme and accountability. The issue of water pollution is alarming. Following control measures are required to improve the situation :

- Supply of one standard of drinking water throughout the country as in developed countries should be ensured. Standard of water for other domestic uses should also be fixed. Feasibility to have dual pipe supply for drinking water and for other domestic uses separately be explored.
- The urban and industrial effluents should not be allowed in rivers.
- Municipal wastes should not be dumped in open.
- As pesticides used for crops enter surface and groundwater as run-off from crops, the farmers need to be educated for the rational use of pesticides.

- Laboratory facilities and manpower required for water quality control particularly in the metropolitans should be assessed and their availability assured.
- Regular monitoring of the quality of groundwater is essential to identify the source of contaminants.
- Public Awareness Programmes and Street Plays on pollution related issues should be organized.
- Industrialists and slum dwellers, who play a large role in polluting the rivers should be part of decision making process in pollution control programmes. Only senior officials concerned with pollution control work, not their representatives should attend meetings related to pollution control.
- Developing facilities for treatment, recycling and reuse of waste water by an individual or community should be subsidized. Use of bio-degradable dyes and paints used for painting idols during Durga Puja, Dusshera, Ganesh Puja etc. should be encouraged.
- Proper Sanitary landfills should be set up to handle the toxic wastes produced by industries.
- Adequate system for collecting and handling municipal wastes and sewage should be developed.
- All efforts by an individual or community to recharge the groundwater should be subsidized.
- Disposing waste through effluent treatment plant, improving system of transportation of sewage, creation of cesspools and advocating use of bio-pesticides are other measures to control pollution.
- Sewage lines should be kept separate from storm water drains and drinking water sources.
- Involvement of so many agencies to detect contaminants creates confusion. One agency equipped with all infrastructure and testing facilities should be made responsible for overall coordination of water quality.
- Creation of community consciousness and their involvement in pollution control should be ensured.
- Political interference in implementing the water related

issues particularly encroachment of water bodies should be stopped. Encroachment of water bodies and converting them into land fit for construction is a common practice promoted mostly by politicians.

- One way to control water pollution is to stop serving bottled water in government sponsored meetings so that they use the same water, common man is using. Why only one group should have the privilege to enjoy bottled water at the cost of public money.
- Innovative approaches used to clean sewage water in few metropolitans like Mumbai and Nasik should be replicated. The purification system called Bio-sanitiser, invented by Malad – resident (Maharashtra) V.S. Shenai wherein sewage water is purified within seconds and is cost-effective should be promoted.

6

Water Crisis and Water Woes

There has always been hunt for water but it is becoming more frantic now. In a report "Charting Our Water Future" issued in 2009, a global deficit of 40 per cent is expected by 2030. Countries with fresh water resources of 1,000 to 1,600 cubic meters per capita per year face water stress. Countries with less than 1,000 cubic meters per capita per year annual internal renewable water resources are considered water scarce. One-third of World's population live in countries under scarce water supply. Below this threshold, water availability is considered a severe constraint on socio-economic development health status and environment. The situation becomes more acute in drought years. India has nearly one-third of the world's water resources with the largest volume of river flow and rainfall which is more than that of the entire continent of Europe put together. In spite of vast water resources, India has reached to an alarming situation in water availability. An annual precipitation of 1,170 mm (average of Cherrapunji – 11,000 mm and Jaisalmer 200 mm) makes India one of the wettest country in the world. The country has failed to manage the finite water resources. The annual per capita availability of fresh water in the country has shrunk alarmingly. With projected increase in population and mismanagement, the per capita water availability by the year 2025 is likely to slip below the danger mark of 1,000 cubic meters. Majority of people are surviving below this limit. In about 60 years of Independence, a water rich nation has been reduced to a water in-secure nation. Predictions of water scarcity arise from estimates of water availability to meet different types of demands. Drinking, cooking and personal hygiene are basic requirement and may not put much pressure on water resources. Other uses like agriculture, industry, tourism, urbanization and sanitation systems with increasing population generate unmanageable demands that aggravate the water crisis. The efforts so far made to find supply-side answers could not sustain in long-run. The main reasons of water scarcity in the country are described below.

Groundwater Depletion

According to Planning Commission Report, 634 Billion Cubic Meters (BCM) is the total water used from underground resources of which 432 BCM is annually replenishable. The rate of extraction of groundwater exceeds the rate of recharge in many blocks in the country. Delhi is at the top in overextraction (78%), followed by Punjab (75%), Rajasthan (59%), Haryana (49%) and Tamil Nadu and Karnataka both at 37 per cent. Growing of water intensive crops and availability of subsidized or free power in many states have resulted in overexploitation of water for irrigation that consumes about 80 per cent of groundwater resources. Urbanization, industrialization and increased population have put huge pressure on water and to meet it one has to go for overextraction of groundwater. According to a report from National Aeronautics and Space Authority (NASA), the groundwater level in Northern India (Haryana, Punjab, Rajasthan and Delhi) is decreasing at the alarming rate over the past decade which is faster than natural recharge process. In many places, borings are drying and re-boring is unsuccessful due to fast decline in water table. One-fourth of the country is moving towards deserts, particularly vast areas in U.P, Bengal, Orissa and Maharashtra. Increase in extraction structures (bore wells, tube wells etc.) from 4 million in 1951 to nearly 20 million at present without needed recharge and conservation efforts has resulted in deepening of wells, thereby increasing pumping lifts, investments and energy costs, arsenic toxicity and salinity.

Surface Water Depletion

The country is fast losing its water resources. A large number of river streams, canals, ponds and tanks have been either encroached upon or have turned into garbage dumps over past few decades. The people have become insensitive to understand the natural hydrological cycle, unscrupulous withdrawing fresh water from aquifer without recharging the aquifers and protecting and conserving the surface water bodies are no body's concerns. The surface water bodies, mainly around urban villages with little or no sewer facilities, have become the recepticles of the wastes like garbage, sewer and effluents that diminishes their water storage capacity and water quality.

Over the last 200 years, the country has either lost or reduced storage capacity of more than one million big and small traditional water harvesting resources and wetlands due to poor maintenance, siltation, indiscriminate construction of big concrete dams and other infrastructure. The area irrigated through tanks and other non-conventional sources has decreased from 21 per cent in 1958-59 to 6.8 per cent in 1991-92.

The distribution of river water resources potential in the country varies (availability in Brahmaputra and Barak is as high as 16,589 cum while it is as low as 360 cum. in Sabarmati basin) as against the national per capita annual availability of water as 2208 cum Brahmaputra and Barak basin with 7.3 per cent of geographical area covering 4.2 per cent population of the country has 31 per cent of the annual water resources. Any situation of less than 1000 cum availability per capita is considered by international agencies as scarcity conditions. Yamuna River, which is a major source of water in the country is today a filthy choked drain with thousand of tonnes of sewage and industrial effluents being poured into it. The condition of other rivers both in flow and quality of water is equally pathetic.

One of the causes of water crisis is too much deforestation. Deforestation because of its direct relationship with rainfall affects the groundwater level: More forests-more rains, more rains-more groundwater. Deforestation affects water resources in two ways: (1) forests and hills are perennial source of water in rivers and falls, with deforestation such supply is reduced, (2) deforestation leads to soil erosion as a result rainwater carries soil to rivers resulting in silt deposition and ultimately reduction in water storage capacity of rivers.

Misuse of water in recent years is another reason of water crisis. We do not value the water. We consider it a free commodity and a natural resource. Water is life and its denial is to deny life. That we waste more water for domestic purpose, for industries and for agriculture is an established fact. Cultivation of water intensive crops like paddy in Punjab and Haryana which were not the crops of these areas resulted in a constant demand for more and more water. Free or subsidized electricity in many states had led to flooding of fields with water, resulted in waterlogging and salinity problems. Benefit of subsidy whether on electricity for agriculture or on water delivery system has failed to reach the poor. Elite class and progressive farmers most of the time are beneficiaries of such subsidies.

According to UN World Water Development Report, released in Mexico in March, 2006, mismanagement, bureaucratic inertia and corruption are the underlining reasons for India's policy failure on water. A few naked facts of corruption highlighted by them are: (1) tempering with water meter readings, (2) bribing for new connection, repair work or for approval of a project on water, sanitation or on irrigation. Lack of political will and inequitable distribution of water are other reasons of water crisis.

Water Wastage in Urban Areas

Water wastage is more in urban areas. Seven mega cities in the country waste between 13 and 53 per cent of treated water. Delhi tops the list, wasting more than 50 per cent of treated water. Another metropolitan city, Chennai lets off nearly 2,58,880 cubic litres of water to the sea every year which is more than its annual requirement of 2,46,375 cubic litres. Leakage, theft, misuse and overuse are main reasons. 30 per cent of potable water in urban areas gets flushed through the toilets which is equivalent to about 250 MGD. The Delhi being the national capital and claims to be a world class city is facing serious problems of water crisis. The important issues and reasons for the water crisis in Delhi are given below :

1. Growing population, increasing industrialization and urbanization coupled with poor management of water resources are main reasons of present water crisis. In spite of several schemes on rainwater harvesting, two-third of rainwater flows in the sea. Out of the total annual precipitation of about 4000 Billion Cubic Meters (BCM), the annual availability of water is about 1120 BCM in the country.
2. Construction of *pucca* roads, flats, industrial establishments and government offices has left very little open *kachcha* space through which surface water can percolate into the ground. Such concrete expansion covering about 370 square kms of agricultural area has deprived of 89 MGD groundwater recharge through seepage if the city gets normal rainfall of 60 cm in the monsoon. Further, construction work in ridge area and in the Yamuna basin has adversely affected and would continue to affect groundwater recharge.
3. Of the total water produced in Delhi (730 MGD), 345 MGD (about 50%) is leaked through different sources like water treatment plants, through pipelines and theft directly from the pipelines. 30 per cent of rainwater along with industrial and household effluents goes as waste in gutter, 60 per cent rainwater is drained in sea through river and hardly 10 per cent rainwater is harvested for domestic and other uses.
4. Delhi Jal Board (DJB) supplies about 6 MGD water through tankers (both DJB's and private tankers). Black marketing by private tanker owners and unconcern-ness of DJB are main hurdles in ensuring water supply. Installation of GPS system in Board's tankers also failed to check the pilferage.

5. Over three lakh illegal booster pumps pull out water before it reaches the residents located at the end of network.
6. Unequal distribution like - 29 litres per capita per day of water supply in some areas compared to 500 litres per capita per day in VIP areas (much above the national standard - 130 litres per person per day) is responsible for water crisis. Unplanned withdrawal of groundwater adds to the problem.
7. Other reasons of diminishing water supply and deterioration in water quality are contamination of water ways and undergroundwater by untreated sewage and waste water discharge. About 800 water bodies (ponds, lakes, baolis etc.) in Delhi because of their heavily silting, being used as garbage dumps and their encroachment have resulted in drastic reduction in storage capacity and ultimately poor recharge of groundwater. Opening of sewage drains in several water bodies have polluted both surface and groundwater. Delhi contributes 80 per cent of total Yamuna pollution. More than 50 per cent (384 MGD) of Delhi's total domestic sewage (710 MGD) discharged untreated is the main cause of Yamuna pollution.
8. A number of agencies like Delhi Government, MCD, DDA, DJB have failed to address water related issue. Rather each of the agencies blames each other on failure. The problem is more of mismanagement.

WATER WOES

Water has been a cause of dispute from time immemorial. Abrahim and later his son, Issac clash with Abilmelech, the king of Philistines over the ownership of wells. The war between Vijayanagar and the Bahamanis over the fertile Raichur doab is well known. Widespread disputes, conflicts and riots on water have been a serious concern world over. Conflicts on water are mainly where rivers and lakes are shared by more than one country or one state. The Nile, the Jordan, the Indus, the Ganga, the Brahmaputra and the Mekong are some of the rivers passing through more than one country. Conflict between Egypt and Ethiopia is on sharing of water of Blue Nile. Israeli - Palestinian conflict is also linked to the water scarcity in the Palestinian areas. By 2025, most of the West Asian countries - Egypt, Libya, Tunisia, Afghanistan, Pakistan and South Africa including India and China will face absolute water scarcity which is defined as less than 1,000 cubic meters of water availability per person per year. They will fight for water to meet their needs for domestic, agriculture, industrial and environmental purposes. China's more ambitious project to build series of dams including a hydel power generation plant diverting the Brahmaputra water to arid-north will have serious impact on water availability in several South-East Asian countries like India, Bangladesh, Myanmar, Cambodia, Laos, Vietnam, Thailand etc.

Inter-state and intra-state conflicts on water are common in India. Sharing of Kauvery water between three States (Tamil Nadu, Karnataka and Kerala) of India is a long dispute. The Inter-state Water Dispute Act which was established in 1956 was amended in 2002 to make it more implementable as per the changed scenario. The Kauvery Water Disputes Tribunal was established in 1990 under the Inter-state Water Disputes Act at the specific direction of the Supreme Court to settle long dispute on sharing of Kauvery water between three states. Kauvery is just a part of problem. The four Southern States – Tamil Nadu, Karnataka, Andhra Pradesh and Kerala have also been struggling for years on their rights on the waters of Krishna, Tungabhadra and Godavari. Even Central Government's interventions failed to resolve the dispute. Several regions of the country have seen violent outbreaks over riparian rights. Individual quarrels, community quarrels are on increase over the years. Surging population growth, industrialization, urbanization, change in agricultural practices, overconsumerism, environmental abuse, and poor management add to the water woes. The problem is severe. Centre's interventions did not work. Neither setting up of tribunals, authorities and committees have alleviated the real sufferings of the people. In conflict, everybody suffers. Change in approach and attitude towards importance of water is the key to resolve the problem.

7
Delhi, A City of Acute Water Crisis

The water demand in Delhi is about 1,000 MGD and supply is 670 MGD. Delhi gets raw water from Yamuna, Ganga, Bhakra Beas Management Board and groundwater. The groundwater which is the primary source of water for drinking and irrigation purposes is depleting fast and is unable to meet the demand. The quality is also deteriorating (with high levels of chlorides, sulphides and nitrates) and is not safe for use. According to CII report, Delhi's water table is falling almost 10 feet per annum and has dropped to 350 feet in most places as compared to 30-40 feet at the time of Independence. With a projected population of 25 million in 2025, Delhi would need an additional 1,200 MGD of water which is difficult to meet with existing resources. The water scarcity in newly coming up colonies is acute. The case of Dwarka, the biggest colony in Delhi is cited. MCD supply is less than a hour a day that fulfills 20-25 per cent of demand. The residents are mostly dependent on undergroundwater which is also scarce and of sub-standard quality. With acute shortage of water, the residents have to depend on DJB or private water tankers that charges about Rs. 1000 for a tanker load which is not affordable by everyone, neither sustainable in long-run.

Reasons of Water Crisis

The Delhi being the mirror of the country and claims to be a world class city is facing serious problems in managing the water crisis. The main reasons for the present crisis are mentioned below:

- Growing population, increasing industrialization and urbanization coupled with poor management of water resources.
- Construction of *pucca* roads, flats, industrial establishments and government offices has left very little open *kachcha* space through which surface water can percolate into the ground. In Delhi alone, such concrete expansion covering about 370 square kms of agricultural area has deprived of 89 MGD groundwater recharge through seepage if the city gets normal rainfall of 60 cm in the monsoon. Further, construction work in ridge area and in the Yamuna basin has adversely affected and would continue to affect groundwater recharge.
- Of the total water supplied in Delhi (730 MGD), 345 MGD (about 50%) is leaked through different sources like water treatment plants, through pipelines and theft directly from the pipelines. 30 per cent of rainwater along with industrial and household effluents goes as waste in gutter, 60 per cent rainwater is drained in sea through river and hardly 10 per cent rainwater is harvested for domestic and other uses.
- In cities, a new culture i.e. tanker culture was introduced to lift water from one source and supply to areas of water shortage. It was mainly meant for poor in areas where no pipelines exist. On the contrary, more than 80 per cent of tanker water is used by rich people who are paying beyond the specified rates. The purpose for which tankers were introduced has not been served. Rs. 40 crore public money is going in drains. The practice is not sustainable in long run.
- Delhi Jal Board (DJB) supplies about 6 MGD water through tankers (both DJB's and private tankers). Black marketing by private tanker owners and unconcernness of DJB are main hurdles in ensuring water supply.

Installation of GPS system in board's tankers also failed to check the pilferage.

- Over three lakh illegal booster pumps pull out water before it reaches the residents located at the end of network.
- Unequal distribution e.g. 29 litres per capita per day of water supply in some areas compared to 500 litres per capita per day in VIP areas (much above the national standard, 130 litres per person per day) is responsible for water crisis.
- Other reasons of diminishing water supply and deterioration in water quality are contamination of waterways and undergroundwater by untreated sewage and waste water discharge. About 800 water bodies (ponds, lakes, baolis etc.) in Delhi because of their heavily silting, being used as garbage dumps and their encroachment have resulted in drastic reduction in storage capacity and ultimately poor recharge of groundwater. Opening of sewage drains in several water bodies have polluted both surface and groundwater. Delhi contributes 80 per cent of total Yamuna pollution. More than 50 per cent (384 MGD) of Delhi's total domestic sewage (710 MGD) discharged untreated pollutes the Yamuna.

Dozens of Schemes Provide no Respite to Water Crisis

Billions of rupees spent on water related projects did not provide any respite to Delhites. A number of projects initiated by Delhi Government to provide relief to water crisis are : (1) dual pipe supply system, (2) zero run-off drainage, (3) recycling waste water, (4) regulating groundwater extraction, (5) checking water theft and (6) pollution control. In addition, a number of programmes have been taken up to address the issues: (1) Installation of Sonia Vihar water treatment plant to supply 140 MGD water to South and East Delhi, (2) Cementing of 'kachcha' Munak canal to save 80 MGD water for water treatment plants at Bawana, Okhla and

Dwarka, (3) Construction of Renuka dam in Himachal Pradesh to provide 275 MGD water to Delhi, (4) Kishan dam and Lakhwar Vyasi dam in Uttaranchal to provide 275 MGD and 135 MGD water respectively, (5) Installation of 4 water recycling plants for utilizing 40 MGD water which otherwise is discarded as waste water generated during water treatment operations, (6) Construction of 50 underground reservoirs to augment water supply and (7) DJB's Interceptor Sewage Treatment Project to clean Yamuna. Many projects are yet to take-off. Most of the plans/policies so far initiated in Delhi have failed to deliver the results. The main reasons are poor execution. A few examples of poor execution and follow-up are given below:

- Delhi Jal Board announced penal action against the misuse and theft of potable water. A provision of fine ranging from Rs. 100 to Rs. 10,000 depending on the offence was imposed. Nine people were challaned for using water illegally by Jal Board in January, 2010. Since January, 2010, hardly any case of water theft has been registered. Not pursuing the plan is one reason of failure.
- The Department of Environment of Delhi Government issued a circular on May 8, 2010 and ordered constitution of an advisory committee at each revenue area to check violations and seal illegal wells, drilling rigs and permanently disconnect water supply. Earlier also the Central Ground Water Authority (CGWA) initiated actions for regulation and control of groundwater resources and imposed ban on digging bore wells. The directions were issued to group housing societies, institutes, hotels, industries and farm houses in the matter. All such efforts became futile because of poor follow-up. However, individual cases were allowed to dig the bore wells with prior permission of Delhi Jal Board or New Delhi Municipal Corporations. The people who have money or are near to power corridors make use of such flexibility and therefore system does not work.

- Spending more than Rs. 40 crore per annum by Delhi Jal Board on tankers has hardly served any purpose. Black marketing and leakage of water from private tankers is rampant. GPS for monitoring the water supply through tankers is almost non-functional. More than 1,100 tankers supply about 6 MGD water daily in Delhi. The tanker water supply is mainly for those areas where no pipelines exist. The system is full of pilferage and the persons for whom the system was introduced are hardly benefited.
- The Delhi Master Plan 2021 whose one of the objectives was to protect the sources of natural water recharge like the Yamuna river basin, vast expanses of agricultural land and the ridge area had hardly been served and would do more damage to the city's water carrying capacity once projected ambitious plans like construction of dams and water treatment plants are executed. Mass construction on the river basin and in the agricultural land of outer Delhi will open the flood gates in Delhi. The city's 370 sq km of agricultural land which has the potential to recharge 89 MGD groundwater, 150 sq km of ridge area which has the capacity to recharge 36 MGD groundwater and 94 sq km of Yamuna flood plain that can recharge 853 MGD groundwater if city gets normal rainfall of 60 cm in the monsoon. Any construction work in these areas would be disastrous. All such works are done in connivance with bureaucrats, politicians and builders' lobby. The situation is becoming bad to worse over the years. It is time to wake up now. There is no use of digging the well when there is fire. Our approach is myopic.

Strategies to Overcome the Water Crisis

In spite of innumerable policies and programmes in last 2-3 decades, there seems to be no respite in water crisis. We simply talk of water conservation techniques, judicious use of water and recycling techniques but we never practice. The present water crisis is our own creation. According to an estimate, we use more than three times the quantity of water than is actually required. Delhi may become a city of acute water scarcity if water related issues are not addressed in a focussed manner. All the efforts should aim for sustainable development and quality improvement of water resources. Rainwater harvesting, groundwater recharge, judicious use of water, avoiding water waste and recycling of waste water are important steps to address the water crisis.

A slewth of majors using individual and community-based approaches are given below :

Community-based Approach

- Harvesting rainwater from roof tops, from run-offs of local catchments, seasonal flood waters and local streams.
- Roof top rainwater harvesting should be made mandatory in every house and colony or in any project exceeding Rs. 25 lakhs.
- Repair, Renovation and Restoration (RRR) of water bodies. The water bodies should be cleared of encroachments.
- Planting canopy of trees on both sides of the road having width of 18 meters or more and keeping central verge (of about 1 meter width) of road *kachcha* for improving groundwater percolation.
- Installing a hydraulic model, a satellite map of the pipelines for constant monitoring of pressure in the water system to prevent leakage.
- Providing sewer lines in all the colonies to stop untreated sewage flow directly into the river.
- Dual pipe supply system to have separate lines for potable and non-potable water.
- Introducing a Bill for regulating groundwater extraction.
- Introducing an intelligent system like GPS to check water theft and control leakages.

- Recycling of residential waste water through water treatment plants. Installation of waste water recycling system in all non-residential buildings having a discharge of 10,000 litres per day should be made mandatory. 50 per cent of the total expenditure can be subsidized by the government.
- Replacing rusty iron pipes and leaking pipe lines with leak proof PVC pipes and installing meters to record bulk supply and individual consumption.
- Empowering local bodies to manage water distribution.
- Ensure that the water which drains into the water bodies is properly treated before its release.
- Municipal wastes should not be dumped in open. The sewage and industrial effluents should be allowed in Yamuna only after treatment.
- Introduction of appropriate technology to ensure efficient use of water in the cooling process, controlling pollution, maximizing recycling and reuse. Insist for using water efficient appliances.
- Introduction of drip and sprinkler irrigation for agricultural lands, parks and gardens.
- Make installation of water meter compulsory in each residence. Also introduce competitive water prices, so those consuming more have to pay more.
- Legal action on misuse of water (illegal tapping, theft, use of water for wrong practices, using potable water for non-domestic purposes and on-line booster).
- Imparting timely information to Delhi Jal Board regarding leakage and bursting of pipelines in the city. Keep watch on use of groundwater particularly by big commercial and industrial users.
- Institution of an annual award for innovative practice on rainwater harvesting and artificial recharge.
- Rainwater falling on flyovers and roads covering a wider area mostly concrete should be used for recharging groundwater rather than flowing in the drains.

- Creating mass awareness about importance of water, its conservation and efficient use through Jal Yatras, articles, shows on Doordarshan, talks on All India Radio, puppet shows, street plays and to conduct demonstrations on rainwater harvesting and artificial recharge to groundwater.
- Organizing art and essay competitions and distribution of booklets, leaflets, folders on water conservation for school/college students.
- Organizing training programmes for government officials, voluntary agencies and other professionals on water management.
- There is a need for decentralized system that includes district-wise, block-wise, colony-wise and society-wise representation to execute the plan. Local bodies should be empowered to manage the water distribution in the area of their jurisdiction.

Individual Approach

All of us should save water and use it more efficiently. The responsibility of an individual is not simply to preach sermon about water conservation but to practise religiously. Here are few tips to be observed by each household :

In the Bathroom

- Do not leave the tap running during brushing the teeth, shaving and washing the cloths.
- Judicious use of showers.
- Fill your bathtub only halfway and close it before turning on the water.
- Check water taps, pipelines and toilet tank for leaks. Seal if necessary.
- Internal service pipelines if rusted and corroded should be immediately changed.
- Putting a container filled with water in toilet tank (cistern) can save 1-2 litres of water in each flush or install low flush toilets or switch over to ventilated

improved pit latrines (which is odourless and does not use water).

- Use ashtray or waste basket in the toilet to keep it clean.
- Ensure that all the taps are closed when not in use.
- Intermittent water supply schedule reduces wastage of water.
- Do not use drinking water to clean car and for moping floor.
- Use of water efficient appliances can save as much as 35 per cent water.

In the Garden/Park

- Trees and shrubs with deep root systems should be watered less frequently than shallow rooted plants which require smaller amounts of water more often.
- Most lawns, shrubs, vegetables and flowers need just one inch of water a week. Do not flood them. Water during cool parts of the day to cut down evaporation.
- Use sprinkler and drip irrigation system for watering gardens and lawns.
- Plantation during the spring or fall requires less water with high survival rate.
- Organic manure improves water holding capacity of soil. Mulch acts as a blanket to keep moisture in and helps prevent erosion, soil compression and weeds.
- Check for and repair of leaky hose connections and sprinkler valves.
- Porous paving materials such as brick, granite or gravel help keep water in the garden.
- Water from kitchen and bathing areas should be recycled, treated and used in garden and parks. Delhi Jal Board's Greenhouse Model Policy provides subsidy in establishing recycling mini plant.

In the Kitchen

- Do not leave the water running while washing the dishes. Better to use two buckets, one for washing and another for rinsing the dishes. Use dishwasher only when full. Dishwasher uses as much as 50 litres of water in each complete cycle.

- Do not wash vegetables and fruits in running water. Use a small bucket.
- Do not use running water to thaw frozen foods.
- Run the washing machine only when full and adjust the water level carefully.

8

Water and Socio-economic Development

Water is the most precious natural resource and a universal asset. Water provides life supporting system for human beings, plants and animals. The importance of water to meet various needs can be traced in ancient texts, inscriptions, local traditions and archaeological remains. It is also important for socio-ecological development.

Water and Human Development

There is no subject which is more important for human development than water. Sufficient and quality water is essential for health, food security, energy security and overall socio-economic development. Poverty alleviation programmes and sanitation needs also depend on water. Water is at the root of all forms of poverty in the world. Financial prosperity is based on green wealth and abundant water. Rain is called "Rahmat" by inhabitants of arid zones world over. The situation is more grave in Asia which has more than half the human population and has less fresh water availability (3,920 cubic meters per person) than any other continent except Antarctica. One-third of world population is facing problems of shortage and poor quality water.

We are dreaming that India would be a developed country in 21st century. Are we preparing for that where there is no water for drink and other domestic use, agricultural production and industrial development. Our ponds are vanishing, rivers are shrinking and polluted, wells are drying and groundwater is depleting at a alarming rate. The poor people are snatched of their water, land and jungles. Other crisis is water pollution and for that industrial effluents, use of chemicals in agriculture, and overextraction of groundwater are responsible. Many of our rivers, wetlands and bays are degraded due to polluted surface run-off and storm water flushed into them.

Water is prime mover in human development. Its crisis is throwing the family budget haywire. Water which is considered a natural resource is not free now. Many a times purchase of bottled water whose cost is almost equal to the cost of milk becomes a necessity. Water quality sometimes is so bad and unfit even for washing, watering the plants and even for construction work and as a safeguard, people use filtered water that costs sometimes equal to the amount of money spent on food. Water scarcity and its poor quality leads to several problems in day to day life. Its crisis affects both the economy and the quality of life. Millions of man hours are wasted everyday to fetch water from long distances. Poor quality water leads to disease outbreaks, malnourishment, crop failure and overall human development. Water has been linked to millennium development goals of poverty alleviation and optimal, equitable and sustainable economic development. Excessive groundwater mining results in decline in water levels, drying up of perennial streams, demise of deep rooted phreatophytes and ground fissuring. In the long-run even irrigated agriculture and industries cannot be sustained. Water crisis affects school attendance, particularly the girls. According to a World Bank Report if water taps are provided closer to the village, school attendance can be increased by about 20 per cent. Saline and brackish water with high hardness contents is disastrous for construction work. These salts seep into concrete, corrode it and rust even steel, thus shortening the life span of buildings. Multi-storied buildings are more prone to danger during moderate seismic activity. A World Bank study says the environmental damage particularly due to polluted water costs India $ 9.7 billion or 4.5 per cent of GDP. Water crisis may lead to a situation of ecological cycle breakdown and the affected regions may face into an endless cycle of droughts, famines, floods and cyclones. Better water management may ward off the perils of 2025.

Water and Health

Water is one of the six basic nutrients viz., carbohydrate, protein, fat, vitamin, mineral and water that are essential for life. A person can survive about a month without food but not more than a week without water. That is the power of water that keeps us healthy and happy. Human body has 70 per cent water. That comes to about 40 litres in our body. We lose water through respiration, perspiration and waste elimination. This loss is to be replaced regularly to keep our body hydrated. Drinking at least 2-3 litres of water is necessary to maintain body water. Dehydration can bring the human body to a grinding halt. A loss of 4-5 per cent body water will mean a 20-30 per cent decline in work performance, 10 per cent loss will cause circulatory failure and with 15 per cent loss, survival is impossible. Not only quantity but quality is equally important. Water pollution is the cause of several water borne diseases. One out of seven diseases and one out of 16 deaths are caused due to polluted water. The common diseases due to polluted water are cholera, diarrhoea, hepatitis, typhoid, amoebic and bacillary dysentery, hydrated cysts, guinea worms etc. Pesticides are worst water pollutants. Prolonged consumption of water contaminated with pesticides may cause cancer, liver and kidney damage, neurological and reproductive disorders. The young children are more sensitive to the effects of pesticides in water.

According to an UN Report, polluted water kills more people than all forms of violence. Every year across the world, more than 3 million people die of water borne diseases. More than 10 lakh people particularly children die due to diarrhoea and dysentery every year in South-East Asia alone. According to WHO Report, more than one million people do not have access to safe and adequate drinking water and water related diseases are the main cause of death for children below 5 years of age. 95 per cent of the natural disasters are water related and are likely to increase with population increase, global warming and overconsumerism. Water crisis is more acute in India. Millions of young children particularly girls in rural India go miles long to fetch water. According to WHO estimates almost one million children in India die because of unsafe drinking water every year. Almost 80 per cent of diseases such as diarrhoea, typhoid, cholera, gastro-enteritis and hepatitis A&C in rural India are caused by water. Based on a survey by WHO in 2000, only 92 per cent urban population and 86 per cent rural population in India get clean water. These figures have drastically reduced over last one decade. According to a World Bank Report, the health impact of India's annual environmental degradation is nearly 10 billion of which 60 per cent is due to water pollution. The problem of contaminated water and intermittent supply when pipes remain empty is more. Empty pipes suck contaminates and provide a breeding ground for germs. The life of pipes and other assets also comes down significantly in an intermittent supply situation. For India to progress, there is need to ensure highest standards of public health which is possible with optimum supply of quality water.

Water, Agriculture and Food Security

About 75 per cent India's population depends on agriculture and allied sector for their livelihoods. Water is central to agriculture and about 75 per cent of fresh water available from different sources is used for agriculture. With galloping growth of population, the water requirement in agricultural sector would further increase to meet the additional needs of agricultural produce. 70 per cent of water used in agriculture goes waste due to poor management. The future lies in sustainable improvement in water productivity, water availability, water conservation and water utilization.

Indian agriculture is 35 per cent irrigated and 65 per cent rainfed. The main source of water for irrigated agriculture is underground and canals. The farmers mostly use tube wells to extract groundwater. In 1994, there were 6.7 million tube wells in India whose number in last 15 years has increased to about 25 million. Nearly 60 per cent of nation's food production depends on groundwater. According to a recent study in America, one foot fall in groundwater level every year over the past decade would have serious implications on agricultural production, food security and overall economy of the country.

India has potential to irrigate 102 million hectares of land until the end of March, 2007 which should exceed to about 120 million hectares by the end of Eleventh Plan (2007-12) to achieve the millennium goals to reduce hunger and poverty. More area under irrigation means more water requirement that would further add to the water crisis. Irrigation would also have a profound impact on nature, local communities and other users of water. Therefore, efforts should be to conserve water and use it more judiciously. Improved water and irrigation management practices can provide new insights into irrigation performance. Water management based on "Principle of More Crop from One Drop" is 'Mantra for the success'.

Green revolution gains which were around Indo-Gangetic plain and mainly dependent on irrigation could not sustain in long-run. China also experienced irrigated agriculture un-economic. In competition for water, domestic and industries will get priority over the agriculture. Rainfed agriculture which constitutes 65 per cent of agriculture in our country will therefore prove more realistic in long-run.

9

Water Conservation and Rainwater Harvesting

Water is the biggest natural resource on earth. There should be balance in its use with nature and human activities. Water conservation should be based on principle of 'Catch water where it falls'. There is need for developing integrated and environmentally sound approaches for water conservation and utilization. The water use efficiency needs to be stepped up. 'Give and take' is the general rule of life. The same applies to water. If you harvest rainwater, store it, recharge groundwater and use it efficiently, it will continue infinitely. Therefore, for sustainable water availability, the efforts should focus on water harvesting, storing, recycling and adopting water saving technologies.

Per capita availability of water depends on its storage capacity that varies greatly between countries. India amongst the semi-arid countries has the lowest capacity to store water. Its per capita storage capacity is 213 cubic meters (m^3) as against 4,733 m^3 in Australia, 1,964 m^3 in the United States and 1,111 m^3 in China. The reservoirs in India can store less than 180 days worth of average flow as compared to reservoirs in the world that can store more than 800 days of average flow. The need for storage will grow with climate change, variability in rainfall and other extreme events including to meet greater demand of water with population growth, urbanization, industrialization and more area under irrigated agriculture.

Water conservation systems in various forms were prevalent in India since ancient times. Numeric references of such practices are available in Vedas and other ancient scriptures. Over a period of time, these systems have undergone refinements and modifications as per location specific needs of the people. 'Rigveda' mentioned a lot about the national and judicious use of water for agriculture, domestic and other purposes. The importance of conserving water to mitigate the natural calamities of droughts and floods has been amply emphasized in the ancient scriptures. Even in 'Arthsastra', Kautilya mentioned the importance of water. Constructing dams, reservoirs, wells and ponds to store water was almost a ritual. An organized water pricing system was in place during the period of Chanakya 3rd - 4th century B.C. Water cannot be produced, but it can certainly be conserved and made available through natural resources like river, groundwater or through rain/melting of snow. The efforts should be to revive, propagate and update our traditional wisdom of harvesting water.

Water conservation plan works on (1) efficient management of rainwater and its storage, (2) allocation and transfer of stored water for use, (3) measures to keep water clean and free from pollution, (4) distribution and consumption with minimum losses and (5) efficient use through adoption of water saving technologies in domestic, agricultural and industrial use. Overall efforts should be to impound surface water with minimum flow to the sea and sustainable exploitation of groundwater, through individual/community and/or public/government initiatives. Most of the initiatives like watershed management, rainwater and groundwater harvesting, judicious use of water in households, agriculture and industries and appropriate recycling techniques due to one or the other reasons did not provide much relief to water crisis. Construction of mega dams has also failed to provide sustainable relief. The concept based on "small is beautiful", may do wonders. Revival and renovation of existing infrastructures/water resources, tapping of existing smaller irrigation canals and sub-soil streams of dry river beds, increasing capacity of pre-existing summer storage tanks, infiltration wells, water treatment plants, construction of overhead reservoir and ground level reservoirs may bring a drastic change. Concreting canals which put an end to water loss through breaches in the canal wall have proved successful to reduce horrific canal loss and therefore augmenting water availability.

Preservation of Water Bodies

Since time immemorial, ponds and other water bodies in villages and towns in the country were the potential sources of water to meet day to day domestic and other requirements of water. Almost total rainwater was drained in these water bodies. Silting and vanishing of these water bodies and their replacement with buildings, roads and agricultural land have deprived country of potential water resources and led country from water surplus stage to a water deprivation stage. As a result, not only groundwater table has fast depleted but the quality of both groundwater and surface water has also deteriorated. Ponds are either created of its own or man-made. They do not require heavy expenditure. According to a study if we convert 3 per cent of our land in ponds, country's water crisis will be over. The work is simple, does not require outsourcing of expertise and can be done using local experience in a participatory mode. State Governments with involvement of Gram Panchayats may play a lead role in reviving and restoring the water bodies.

Groundwater Recharge

Groundwater which is about 22 per cent of total potable water on the earth is a potential source of water for different purposes. Fast declining of groundwater level is a serious concern and needs to be addressed on priority. The solution lies in recharging of groundwater to stabilize the flow as well as arrest contamination. Groundwater is not an endless resource. We have to be careful in its use. Any withdrawal has to be replenished. It is like a bank account where a minimum amount is required for opening an account. That becomes the reserve money in the bank. Subsequent withdrawal depends on the amount deposited. Similarly extraction of groundwater should depend on how much water is recharged in the ground. Any withdrawal without recharging the groundwater would lead to loss of reserve water and a day will come, your reserve of groundwater will be closed like your bank account is closed when you withdraw the total amount. We are heading towards that stage. The real long-term solution lies in a decentralized water conservation approach along with optimum utilization of the available rainwater and groundwater in the drought affected regions. Imperative measures for groundwater recharge include restriction on its excess extraction for cash and water intensive crops. Recharging approach is simple, does not involve big budget, no bureaucratic and unwieldy planning. It can be implemented by peasants. Only willpower and commitments are required. To check the depletion of groundwater aquifers the Government has constituted an Artificial Recharge or Groundwater Advisory Council to arrest the trend of indiscriminate groundwater extraction.

Water Conservation in Hills

In high altitude areas, bunding of land from hill to valley helps in conserving water, reducing river flow and improving undergroundwater level. Dense plantation in hills can save water and improve soil fertility. Plants may be of food and fruits, fuelwood, building wood, animal feed and fiber trees. Trees like eucalyptus that absorbs huge moisture from the soil should be avoided. Upstream storage of water by building huge reservoirs help trap the silt before the water travels to the down-stream and prevent problem of silt in Himalayan Rivers. The upstream storage facility also keeps in regulating water supply during the lean period for maintaining uninterrupted power supply throughout the year. Water scarcity in hills where glaciers are the only source of water, has been a life-long challenge. Ladakh is rain-shadow areas of Himalaya where the average rainfall seldom exceeds 50 mm. The only water available to the people in that region is through melting of glaciers in summer. Building of artificial glaciers that provides relief to the farmers in such areas needs to be promoted.

Efficient and Sustainable use of Water

The estimated utilizable annual water resources are about 1,122 billion cubic meters, out of which we have been able to use only 605 billion cubic meters i.e. about 50 per cent of the resources and remaining 50 per cent goes as waste. Our efforts should be to utilize the balance resources in a sustainable manner. There is enough water if we use it carefully. Increasing population, urbanization, industrialization and changing cropping pattern demand more water and may lead to detrimental effects on the environment, society and the economy if we do not use water more sparingly. It requires a behavioural change, assigning a value to water and use it more efficiently. Everybody should have a responsibility to save water. Stop wasting water. Conserve whenever possible. Use technologies like front loading washers, low flow faucets and showerheads and water conserving toilets to conserve water. Water harvesting approach as a movement, water literacy drive, better data management, decentralization and equity may provide relief to water crisis. In urban areas, the multiple agencies controlling water supply and water use with lack of clarity and proper planning have been an utter failure.

Water Conservation in Rural India

Rural India is facing water crisis too. Clean, green and open environment is disappearing from the villages. Traditional water resources like wells and ponds are vanishing. Deforestation is rampant. Open area is diminishing. There is need for multifaceted approach to revive past glory of Indian villages. Followings are suggestive approaches :

1. All traditional water resources need repair, cleaning and de-silting. The work should be initiated with

involvement of Self-Help-Groups (SHGs) and Government support for need based funds for digging and their subsequent maintenance.

2. Green (forest) area in each village should be increased. Villages should be involved in plantation as forest department has been a failure. In case of dispute between forest department and villagers on forest area, the land should be given to villagers with the conditions that they use it for plantation of trees.
3. Area under irrigated agriculture should be restricted and decided as per water availability. Intensive cropping particularly cash crops may prove hazard in long-run.
4. Restricting installation of industries that require heavy demand of water in areas where water is already scarce.
5. Involve people who are involved with water related issues and have long experience in water conservation programme.
6. Avoiding water waste by installing pipelines, water taps including repair of breakages in irrigation channels and drains.
7. There are water surplus regions and water deficit regions. Efforts should be to conserve surplus water in storage structures or to transmit it to water deficit regions through conveyance systems.
8. To start community based rainwater harvesting and watershed development programmes to meet agricultural and drinking water needs.

RAINWATER HARVESTING

Rain is primary source of water whereas rivers, lakes and groundwater are all secondary sources of water. With the change in lifestyle, we now mostly depend on secondary sources of water and in the process, we have forgotten that rain is the ultimate source that feeds all these secondary sources. Such ignorance for long-time is the main cause of water crisis.

Rainwater harvesting traces its history to Biblical times. Rainwater harvesting technology existed 4000 years ago in the Palestine and Greece. In ancient Rome, residences were built with individual cisterns and paved courtyards to capture rainwater from city's aqueducts. Farming communities in Baluchistan impounded rainwater as early as the third millennium B.C. The rural habitations of India used to meet household water requirement by the traditional methods of collecting rainwater locally in community ponds, diverting and storing water from local streams/springs and tapping sub-surface water below river/stream beds since the dawn of civilization. These basic techniques have been successfully applied by the people in different parts of the country in different ways. All these methods are eco-friendly and can be adopted at affordable cost to meet the needs especially in agricultural crop production by the farmers.

India is one of the wettest regions in the world. Annual rainfall is still 1170 mm contrary to America where the annual rainfall is hardly 200 mm. Take case of Cherapunji where annual rainfall is 1100 cm. the highest in the world, and people suffer from serious drinking water shortages within 2-3 months after the rains. Is it the water conservation approach in our country? The main cause of water scarcity lies in our wrong approach of water use. We rely more on the use of surface and groundwater rather than rain and flood waters which are available in abundance. India gets an estimated 400 million hectares of rain and snowfall but no real efforts are made to tap this enormous resource.

What is Rainwater Harvesting?

Rainwater harvesting means capturing rains where it falls or capturing the run-off in the particular area. To keep water clean by not allowing its pollution in the catchment is equally important and part of rainwater harvesting. The rainwater collected can be stored for direct use or can be recharged into the groundwater.

Why is Rainwater Harvesting Important in India?

India receives most of its rainfall in just 100 hours out of the 8,760 hours in a year as compared to Western countries where rainfall hours are manyfold. High rainfall (> 1100 mm per annum) in a short span of time in India overflow and drain through rivers in the sea for want of proper harvesting and storage devices. This is the reason, country is facing acute water scarcity. Long neglect of water conservation approaches including rainwater harvesting has led to groundwater depletion and reduction in storage capacity of surface water resources. Rainwater harvesting therefore, is essential (1) to recharge groundwater to replenish the groundwater extraction loss and (2) to store and augment surface water resources for future use.

How much Water can be Harvested?

The total amount of water that is received in the form of rainfall over an area is called the rainwater endowment of the area. Out of the total rainfall, the amount that can be effectively harvested called the water harvesting potential. Water harvesting potential depends on rainfall and collection efficiency. The loss due to evaporation, spillage including first flush wastage are considered in estimating the collection efficiency. Normal collection efficiency is 60 per cent of total rainfall. The volume of water harvested depends on (1) area of plot, (2) height of rainfall and (3) collection efficiency. Rainwater harvesting under rural and urban scenario as a whole has been computed and given below.

Computation of Rainwater Collection Potential in Rural Area

India's total land area is about 300 m ha. Out of which inaccessible land area where from rainwater cannot be harvested is 100 m ha., leaving therefore 200 m ha. land area suitable for rainwater harvesting. Assuming 6 lakh villages in India and 1200 mm average annual rainfall, the annual endowment of water in the country, in a village and availability per person per annum has been worked out. Factors taken for computation are given below.

Computation of Rainwater Collection Potential

• Total land area of rainfall	300 m ha.
• Total land area where runoff can be harvested	200 m ha.
• Average rainfall in the country	1200 mm
• Annual endowment of water in the country	2.448 m cu km
• Assuming 6 lakh villages in India, the runoff land area accessible to each village	335 ha
• Assuming average population per village as 1200, the average rainwater availability per person per annum	3.4. m. litres
• Average rainwater availably per person per day	9350 litres

Computation of Rainwater Collection Potential in Urban Area (Delhi)

The situation in urban areas, particularly in metropolitan cities like Delhi is different because of per capita land area availability where runoff can be harvested, less rainfall as compared to country's average rainfall and increased water demand. Rainwater collection potential in Delhi based on above conditions can be computed as below :

• Delhi's area	1,500 sq. km.
• Average rainfall	600 mm
• Per cent rainfall that can be harvested	60
• Annual rainwater collected through rains	3.6 lakh million litres

• Delhi's daily water requirement	4,000 million litres
• No. of days harvested water can be used	90

Roof Top Rainwater Collection Potential

For a family residing in a building with flat terrace area of 100 sq. m, rainwater collection potential can be computed using following factors :

• Area of plot	100 sq. m
• Annual rainfall	600 mm
• Effective harvesting rate	60 per cent
• Volume of water harvested	36,000 litres
• For a five number family, domestic water requirement per day (150 litres/person/day)	750 litres
• No. of days harvested water can be used for domestic purpose by the family	48 days

Benefits of Rainwater Harvesting

These calculations show the enormous and undeniable potential of rainwater harvesting to meet domestic and other needs of water. Rainwater harvesting techniques increase groundwater recharge, reduce storm water discharges, urban floods and overloading of sewage treatment and also reduce sea water ingress in coastal area. Rainwater harvesting in urban area particularly reduces demand for municipal corporation water supply and improves groundwater quality. The different surveys revealed that rainwater harvesting could meet the acid test of bad drought.

Rainwater Harvesting Systems

Rainwater is one of the most crucial and traditional approach of water conservation. Two main approaches are used for rainwater harvesting. The first one is storage of rainwater on surface which is a traditional approach. The various structures used in this approach are underground tanks, ponds, check dams and weirs etc. The other approach is groundwater recharge. This approach uses structures like pits, trenches, plug wells, hand pumps, recharge wells, recharge shafts, lateral shafts with bore wells. The various water harvesting systems depending upon the sources of water supply are described below.

Storage of Rainwater on Surface

Community based rainwater harvesting technologies have been the source of people's survival in water scarce areas of rural India. Our ancestors over a long period had learnt to harvest water in number of ways: (1) Harvesting the rain drop directly from roof tops and store it in tanks built in the courtyards, (2) Collecting rainwater from open community lands and store it in artificial wells, (3) Capturing water from swollen streams during the monsoon season and store it in various forms of water bodies and (4) harvesting water from flooded rivers and canals. Since the agro-climatic conditions, topography, the regional hydrogeology, the local traditions and customs vary, it is difficult to prescribe a single rainwater harvesting system for different regions of the country. Any approach without considering above variables will not be sustainable in long-run. Therefore, different options to harvest the rainwater need consideration. An ingenious system of rainwater harvesting known as *Kund* or *Kundis* in the low rainfall areas of Rajasthan, harvesting springs through diversion channels for irrigation in hilly areas and mountainous region and percolation tanks and ponds in Southern India are common approaches. *Jalkunds* (water storage tanks) have been found very useful for sustainable rainwater harvesting especially in the north-eastern hill region. The site of the *Jalkund* is selected at high ridges of crop catchment area to allow direct precipitation during water harvesting period. Before onset of monsoon, the *Kund* is escavated and its bed and lining is smoothened by plastering with mixture of clay and cow dung (in the ratio of 5:1). Lining material like low density polyethylene agri-film is then used to check the seepage loss. Cushioning material such as soft grasses, pine leaves etc. are used below the available water resources to prevent damage to the lining material. Linking ponds and open wells to conserve rainwater are simple and affordable approaches and are most suitable for taking up at community level to harvest rainwater.

Rainwater Recharge to Groundwater

A process by which the groundwater reservoir is augmented at a rate exceeding that obtained under natural conditions is called recharge to groundwater. The structures generally used to recharge the groundwater are mentioned below:

Ponds and Tanks: Conserving rainwater in ponds and tanks and its percolation into groundwater is a cheap and healthy practice of groundwater recharge throughout India.

Pits: Recharge pits are constructed for recharging the shallow aquifer. These are constructed 1 to 2 m. wide and to 3 m. deep which are back filled with boulders, gravels, coarse sand etc.

Trenches: These are suitable for shallow aquifers. Trench may be 0.5 to 1 m wide, 1.5 m. deep and 10 to 20 m. long depending upon availability of water. These are back filled with boulders, gravels, coarse sand etc.

Dug wells: Existing dug wells may be utilized as recharge structure and water should pass through filter material before putting into dug well.

Handpumps: The existing handpumps may be used for recharging the shallow/deep aquifers, if the availability of water is limited. Water should pass through filter media before diverting it into handpumps.

Recharge wells: Recharge wells of 100-300 mm. diameter are generally constructed for recharging the deeper aquifers and water is passed through filter media to avoid choking of recharge wells.

Recharge Shafts: For recharging the shallow aquifer which are located below clayey surface, recharge shafts of 0.5 to 3 m. diameter and 10 to 15 m. deep are constructed and back filled with gravels, coarse sand etc.

Lateral shafts with bore wells: For recharging the upper as well as deeper aquifers lateral shafts of 1.5 to 2 m. wide and 10 to 30 m. long depending upon availability of water with one or two bore wells are constructed. The lateral shafts are back filled with filter material as mentioned above.

Channelizing Rainwater into the Ground: Channelizing rainwater into the ground is simple and least expensive approach. The approach suits both to rural communities and city dwellers. In this approach, the rainwater is channelized directly through plastic pipes into the ground. However, channelizing polluted water under the banner of rainwater harvesting in the groundwater is dangerous and should be avoided.

Rainwater Harvesting Bye-laws

A steep decline in the groundwater table in different parts of the country has been observed in recent years. The situation in urban areas is peculiar. Delhi is under water blues. On one hand, there is acute water scarcity because of spiralling population growth, unplanned urban development associated with large scale industrialization. On the other hand, these are often overflooded with water during the monsoon. This has affected both the quality and quantity of groundwater. Fast depleting groundwater table has virtually put the urban water management in shamble. Water conservation has now become need of the day and the idea of groundwater recharging by harvesting rainwater is being continually emphasized. Town planners and civic authorities all-over the country have introduced by-laws for encouraging rainwater harvesting. Following initiatives have been taken by the Government in recent past :

- Since June 2001, the Ministry of Urban Affairs and

Poverty Alleviation has made rainwater harvesting mandatory in all new buildings with a roof area of more than 100 sq. m. and in all plots with an area of more than 1000 sq. m.

- The Central Ground Water Authority (CGWA) has made rainwater harvesting mandatory in all institutions and residential colonies in notified areas (South and South-West Delhi and adjoining areas like Faridabad, Gurgaon and Ghaziabad). This is also applicable to all the buildings in notified areas that have tube wells.
- The CGWA has banned drilling of tube wells in notified areas.
- Rainwater harvesting has been made mandatory in all new buildings with an area of 200 sq.m or more.
- A rebate on property tax has been offered as an incentive for implementing rainwater harvesting systems.

After installation of rainwater harvesting system was made mandatory in Delhi, Central Ground Water Board (CGWB) filed an affidavit that roads could also harvest rainwater. The work will be taken up at link road from national highway 8 to Dwarka. In spite of all bye-laws and enforcements, the percentage of rainwater harvested is very low. Hardly 10-12 per cent of rainwater is being used, the remaining is drained. Hardly 1 per cent of the buildings with plot area of over 100 square metres have provision of rainwater harvesting system. The execution part in India is mostly on papers.

10

Schemes/Programmes on Water Development

In spite of innumerable schemes/programmes supported by Central and State Governments including World Bank, Asian Development Bank, NGOs and private sector to augment water supply for meeting the agricultural and drinking water needs, the India's per capita water availability has declined to one-third in last 60 years and is projected to fall to one-fourth by 2025. The country is heading towards severe water scarcity. Waterlogged area has increased three-fold in 30 years. Nine river basins nurturing 20 crore population are water scarce. The fresh water availability is constantly under stress. At the same time, the overexploitation in certain areas and un-planned developments have severely affected the quality and sustainability of resources. 80 per cent of 14 perennial rivers are polluted. Lakhs of crores of rupees have been spent without visible results. Where are funds being sucked? What is wrong with our policies? These are certain issues that have been addressed in this chapter.

Schemes/Programmes to Improve Irrigation Potential

The main aim of irrigation programmes is to get optimal productivity per unit of water. The approach should be scientific water management, improved farm practices and sprinkler and drip systems of irrigation.

Ministry of Water Resources, Government of India introduced several Schemes/Programmes to improve irrigation potential in the country. The working group for water resources for the XI plan fixed a target for creation of irrigation potential of 16 million hectares (9 m. ha. through major and medium irrigation projects and 7 m. ha. through minor irrigation projects) against 8.82 m. ha. in X plan. The benefits from major and medium projects that were spectacular in the first 10-20 years, reduced gradually and considerable portions of the land got deteriorated due to waterlogging, soil salinity and alkalinity problems.

Command Area Development Programmes (CADP) was started in 1974-75. It was renamed as Command Area Development and Water Management Programmes (CADWMP) on April 1, 2004. Under CADWMP, central assistance is provided to the State Governments in the form of grants for micro-level infrastructure development and efficient farm management practices (such as construction of field channels, intermediate and link drains, repair of canal systems, training and adaptive trials) for optimizing agricultural productivity and improving socio-economic conditions of farmers. Till now 314 projects have been included covering a command area of 28.65 m. ha. in the scheme. Presently, the programme is on-going in 136 projects spread over 27 States. Under the Accelerated Irrigation Benefits Programme (AIBP), out of 229 water resource projects receiving central assistance, 95 are likely to be completed soon. Recently, Union Government has relaxed the AIBP criteria to attract more project proposals in special category states, tribal and drought prone areas across the country. Farmer's Participatory Action Research Programme through involvement of specialized agencies like Agricultural Universities, ICAR, ICRISAT, Water and Land Management Institute (WALMI) was implemented in 5,000 villages in research oriented mode with an aim to launch massive water literacy drive on water conservation and also envisages implementation of available technologies towards increasing the productivity and profitability of agriculture. An additional 10 m. ha. assured irrigation was targeted under Bharat Nirman Programme. Canal Irrigation Project was launched in 1991 with an aim to increase irrigated land during a 15 years period (1991-2004). The total funds allocated were 1,00,000 crore. The irrigated land from 178 lakh hectare in 1991-92 reduced to 146 lakh hectare in 2003-04 due to poor maintenance, lack of cleanliness and repair work of canals in the project. A micro-irrigation scheme with a budget of Rs. 550 crore was launched in 2007 to improve water use efficiency through drip and sprinkler irrigation.

Average water use efficiency of irrigation projects is about 30 to 40 per cent for canal irrigation and about 60 per cent for groundwater irrigation. The achievements are much below the expectations and do not commensurate with the funds spent on irrigation schemes. The reasons for poor performance of irrigation schemes other than the rampant corruption, political interference and lack of synergy between different departments/agencies are mentioned below :

- Financial crunch faced by most of the States to maintain the distribution systems developed under different schemes with the support of Central Government and other agencies.
- Lack of involvement of stakeholders in the operation, management and maintenance of irrigation system.
- Water Users Association (WUAs) due to internal conflicts and lack of clarity in working are unable to function to its potential.
- Lack of efforts to renovate and upgrade the irrigation system, mitigation of waterlogging and inequity in supply of water to tail-end-reaches and lack of facilities to diagnose the shortcomings in the system and their remedy.
- Poor attention to rehabilitate minor irrigation tanks.
- Inequity in development of water resources and neglecting the disadvantaged regions of the country.
- Non-completion of large number of irrigation and multi-purpose projects in time and spillover from one plan to another.
- Delay in land acquisition, forest clearance and rehabilitation of project affected persons.

Schemes/Programmes to improve Drinking Water Availability

Providing drinking water to all sections of the society, both in urban and rural areas has been the Central Government's top-most priority. Even the National Common Minimum Programme (NCMP) is committed to address water related issues, both for irrigation and drinking purposes by 2010 as a key component of Bharat Nirman Programme. The UPA Government developed a blueprint to revive about 20,000 ponds with ADB loan of Rs. 4,500 crore by 2010. It was expected to irrigate 15 lakh hectare land with revival of 20,000 ponds.

The country in 1978 under a written international agreement promised to provide safe drinking water to each person within 10 years. The promise was not kept in one decade. Then a technology mission was constituted in 1986. Billions of rupees were spent without fulfilling the target to provide safe drinking water. Rajiv Gandhi National Drinking Water Mission was launched by Central Government in 1991 with an aim to provide safe drinking water to local communities including SC and ST. Two agencies namely National Water Commission and Central Ground Water Board were created by the Central Government in 2008 to develop strategies for improving water conservation and water use efficiency. These two agencies were also to provide the requisite assistance to the State Governments with technical inputs. National Water Harvester's Network (NWHN) whose members are primarily professionals, bureaucrats, grassroots level functionaries, interested citizens and those committed in developing or undertaking water harvesting programme addresses and highlights the local issues and the traditional systems relating to water and to further the cause of community based water management. The network did not make any headway.

Schemes/Programmes on Dams and Canals

Despite spending Rs. 1,42,269 crore on dam/canal irrigation

projects between 1990 and 2007, the net area irrigated by canals declined over the years. The canal system is in terminal decline and has failed to offset monsoon vagaries. According to a Government report, there is no actual increase in agricultural production or the irrigated area of the major crops under 10 major irrigation projects built in 13 States. The example of Indira Sagar Dam, the India's largest dam, is cited here. The dam is irrigating only 11 per cent of its potential, a reflection of a system that builds dams but does not finish or maintain the canal system. The story is same across India. Only 27 per cent of the Sardar Sarovar Project's (Eastern Gujarat) distribution network and 23 per cent of the Rengali Project which is 200 km. west of Bhubaneswar are complete. Why is less land irrigated by canals in spite of mega dams is surprising to many? The answer is simple i.e. inadequate treatment of catchment areas, leading to silts in reservoirs. About two-thirds of Indira Sagar and Sardar Sarovar catchments that run into several lakh hectares are yet to be treated. The extent of devastation caused by construction of big dams is main reason of failure, e.g. the Polavarum Dam across the river Godavari with estimated cost of Rs. 17,000 crore has been cleared by Ministry of Environment in July, 2010 with expected irrigated area of 2.91 lakh hectares and power generation 960 MW at the cost of inundating parts of Andhra Pradesh, Orissa and Chhattisgarh, swamping 280 villages and displacement of 2 lakh people mostly tribals. Imagine a tsunami of 200 thousand million cubic feet of dam water breaking across the Godavari delta in case there is flood in Godavari. Overnight, 45 lakh people would have a water grave.

Schemes/Programmes on Rivers

India is a land of many rivers: 14 big rivers, 55 medium rivers and hundreds of small rivers that cover an area of about 329 million hectares. The total river length is approximately 45,000 kilometers that cater needs of 80 per cent of the country's population. Millions of people, particularly rural and agriculture oriented in the country depend on rivers for their livelihoods and sustenance.

The rivers once considered the spiritual lifeline and source of sustenance are no more than the filthy drains in India. Rivers like Ganga, Yamuna and Sabarmati are among top polluted rivers. The other rivers like Damodar in Bengal, Chalia in Calicut, Hoogli in Kolkata, Son in Bihar, Godavari in Andhra Pradesh, Kuan in Chennai, Kullu in Mumbai are equally polluted. Water extraction, dam construction and pollution are killing Indian rivers. The major sources of pollutants are waste water from urban areas. Garbage along the river side, discharge of chemical and industrial waste water, including idols during Dusshera, Durga Puja and Ganesh Chaturthi, dumping of carcasses (dead animals), half and unburnt human remains, flow of pesticides and insecticides from farmland are dumped in the rivers. The level of pollution in few rivers is very high. Persistent high contaminants from river system to ground aquifers has made the groundwater unfit for consumption. It is not only river pollution but slow or stagnant river flow is a big hurdle for ensuring both clean and continuous flow of rivers. The hydel projects on rivers are the main constraints in maintaining the minimum flow. Shrinking of river width and change in their course due to habitation and construction activities at the river basin is rampant. The width of Yamuna in its 22 km. course in Delhi has reduced to half km. from 3.5 km. in last 60 years.

Several projects have been sanctioned for harnessing and reviving the rivers. Two decades old National River Conservation Programme in spite of spending more than Rs. 5,000 crore did not improve the health of the critically polluted rivers. An ambitious National River Project launched in 2008 to conserve rivers for improving irrigation and power production potential is yet to take off. An amount of Rs. 817 crore on Ganga Action Plan and Rs. 1,306 crore on Yamuna Action Plan has been spent with no visible improvement. National Ganga River Basin Authority (NGRBA) set up in 2009 for revamping of the river conservation strategy did not make any progress in last one year. Sewage treatment plants established in different cities are working much below their capacity. The need is for focussed and time bound action plan. Unless river pollution is considered a national problem, steps taken by Government including interventions by honourable court will not work. The local communities who depend on rivers must be involved. Children can be a driving force to create awareness. The projects related to clearing rivers are mostly funded by the Central Government but water being a state subject, monitoring of any such project becomes difficult. Declaring some of the most polluted rivers of the country as "National Rivers" will facilitate the centre's direct intervention in projects to clean up such rivers. The "National Rivers" concept mooted in 2006, is yet to take off.

Schemes/Programmes to Revive Water Bodies

A programme for Repair, Renovation and Restoration of Water Bodies was launched by Agriculture Ministry in January, 2005 with a budget provision of Rs. 300 crore. The programme covering 1098 water bodies was implemented in 26 districts in 15 States. 75 per cent of the project cost was extended to States as subsidy. Out of 1098 water bodies targeted in the programme 630 water bodies were completed by the end of 10th plan. The Government in 2006 developed another scheme with Rs. 4,500 crore ADB loan per year for reviving 20,000 ponds. About 15 lakh hectare land could be irrigated with revival of these ponds. Petty support of Rs. 2000 to Rs. 10,000 for constructing water conservation structure like deepening of tanks, ponds and wells by different State Governments has no impact. Such piecemeal support proved as waste of public money. Rivers, lakes and other reservoirs can never be conserved or restored with isolated efforts. The need is for holistic approach at national level covering each and every village of the country.

Schemes/Programmes on Groundwater Recharge

The Central Groundwater Board has prepared a master plan for artificial recharge of groundwater, especially in areas which face water scarcity problems. The total cost of the project is Rs. 24,500 crore (Rs. 19,880 crore for rural areas, Rs. 2.25 crore for urban areas and remaining to meet coordination work). The project to be implemented in phased manner is expected to develop 2.25 lakh artificial recharge structures in rural areas, 37 lakh roof top rainwater harvesting structures in urban areas including 2700 springs in States like Jammu and Kashmir, Himachal Pradesh, Uttarakhand, north-eastern states and Sikkim. 36,453 MCM is estimated annual surplus surface run-off from rainwater in rural areas. To popularize the concept of artificial recharge of groundwater among stakeholders, the Ministry of Water Resources has constituted an Artificial Recharge of Groundwater Advisory Council. The idea is to ensure sustainable development with people's participation in development of water resources.

In spite of imposing ban on groundwater extraction by the Government, the groundwater extraction continues to be a rampant practice. A citizen has a right at least to have optimum level of water. If he does not get that optimal amount, he will explore all possibilities to get it. Hence ban on groundwater extraction has no logic if water is scarce, people are thirsty and dying of water scarcity and with use of polluted water. These are interim arrangements to quench the thirst and will continue till a sustainable solution is available. Rather, efforts should be to augment water availability and metering of water supply both at community and individual level to check and control wastage of water.

In the light of decline of groundwater level at an alarming rate, regulatory directives were issued by the Central Ground Water Authority for 108 severely critical and overexploited groundwater blocks in the country. The regulations were not enforced because of faulty groundwater management policy. One such decision to provide free or subsidized power for groundwater irrigation in many States like Punjab and Haryana proved fatal to groundwater extraction in long-run. Over-extraction of groundwater led to depletion of groundwater level, waterlogging and soil salinity problems. Central Government brought a Model Groundwater (Regulation and

Control) Act twice in 1970 and 1992. Central Government also constituted Central Groundwater Authority to protect over-extraction of groundwater. As water being a state subject, all these acts and authorities become ineffective due to lack of cooperation and synergy between State and Central Government. Other initiatives taken in recent past to create awareness in respect of water related issues and to implement the projects for long-term gains are mentioned below.

National Water Policy, 2002

A National Water Policy initially conceived by National Water Resources Council (NWRC) on 9th September, 1987, was revised, updated and finally adopted by NWRC in April, 2002. The policy has an integrated and multi-disciplinary approach to the planning, formulation, clearance and implementation of the projects. The policy envisages the formulation of a state water policy and preparation of an Operational Action Plan in a time bound manner to achieve the desired objectives. The policy integrates quantity and quality aspects including environmental considerations. It stresses involvement of people in project planning and a participatory approach in water resources management. Ensuring safe drinking water to all habitations by 2012 is ultimate aim of the policy.

Year of Fresh Water, 2003

United Nations in 2003 in its resolution on water related issues declared year 2003 as year of fresh water. The objectives were: (1) to increase awareness among stakeholders about the scarcity of fresh water, (2) conservation and efficient use of fresh water, (3) fresh water quality preservation and (4) augmentation of usable resources. The Government of India as part of United Nations Resolution declared 2003 as fresh water year whose main objective was to create awareness among masses regarding fresh water scarcity and the need for its conservation. Important activities as part of celebrating 'year of fresh water - 2003' included (1) launching of Mass Awareness Programme,

(2) organizing seminars and workshops and (3) expediting schemes on water harvesting and conservation. When did fresh water year start and when did it end, went unnoticed by majority. Neither the impact of the programmes on water conservation and water saving was studied by any agency in a span of one year in the country.

Water Year - 2007

With a view to address water-related issues in a focussed manner, to ensure successful implementation of policies and programmes and to launch a massive awareness programme all-over the country, the Ministry of Water Resources declared the year 2007 as water year. A number of activities for masses, for school/college students, for stakeholders and for professionals were identified to ensure that every drop was judiciously utilized and water conservation movement was adopted by all concerned in letter and spirit.

World Water Day

The World Water Day (WWD), an United Nations sponsored event is celebrated on March 22 every year to address water scarcity issues. The main objectives to celebrate (WWD) are: (1) to develop international co-operation, (2) to create awareness about importance of water and (3) to adopt measures for preventing contamination of water. Every year World Water Day comes and goes. The true spirit of celebrating World Water Day to utilize every drop of water in all walks of life to ensure conservation, preservation and management of water resources is missing. Such declarations are mostly celebrated as rituals and hardly have any visible impact.

Analysing the Reasons of Failure

Water is a sensitive issue. It is life elixir. Therefore, getting water to meet the essential needs is the right of every citizen. Our schemes and policies on water should have been aimed in the light of these considerations. There have been innumerable schemes/policies on water sector both supported by Central and State Governments. The country has spent billions of rupees on water management in last 60 years. More than an amount of Rs. 1 lakh crore on drinking water schemes and more than 1.4 lakh crore on canal/dam irrigation schemes have been spent by the Government alone. In spite of that, there has not been any increase in drinking water availability nor the area under canal irrigation has increased. Rather situation is getting bad to worse over the years. Water crisis cannot be overcome by mega and expensive schemes alone. The Indira Sagar Dam, the India's largest dam irrigating only 11 per cent of the land it is supposed to irrigate, is a reflection of a poor system that builds and manages dams and canals.

Lack of focussed and targeted aims, poor planning, delay in implementation, isolated approach, clash of interest of different agencies involved in the work, no monitoring, evaluation and post-project sustainability plan, no accountability of defaulters, excessive inertia, incompetence, inefficiency, corruption, political interference and wasted interests in the system at all levels are reasons of failure. The issues like participation, incentives, water entitlements, transparency, entry of the private sector, competition, accountability, financing and environmental quality which are not part cf the existing management plan are other reasons of poor performance or failure of the schemes. A few specific reasons are mentioned below.

Ad-hoc Approach to Grant the Schemes

Most of the schemes suffer due to ad-hoc approach. We are in hurry to announce and launch the schemes and even in allocating the funds without assessing the needs, funds availability and implementation plan. I remember an incidence of 1999 when an emergency session of Parliament was convened after restless protesters turn unruly on water issue. One of the measures suggested by the then Government was to import water on emergency basis. Such ad-hoc decisions under pressure without assessing pros and cons of the scheme can never be executed neither sustainable in long-run. Any such approach is simply to calm down the mass and fool the people.

Involvement of Multiple Departments/Agencies Hampers the Progress

Interest of each department/agency differs. Agencies like Central Groundwater Board, Central Water Commission, National River Linking Project, Ganga and Yamuna Action Plans and Ministries like Water Resources Development, Irrigation, Agriculture, Environment and Forest, Rural Development including Central Government and State Governments do not have any synergy in their working. Centre's role is limited to management of crisis like floods, droughts and inter-state disputes. The water being State subject, the concern of the states is simply water, water and water. Involvement of different departments, agencies and Ministries with no clear agenda and role to play simply adds confusion and hampers the progress. Because of involvement of too many departments/agencies, the staffing levels in different schemes on water for the same work are 10 times international norms. This leads to spending most of the public funds under establishment head rather than maintaining the infrastructure and providing needed service.

Top-Down and Fragmented Approach

Government agencies in spite of working for last 6 decades did not make any headway in addressing the water issues. The main reason being top-down approach. Most of the schemes are developed in national/state capital(s) and planning commission(s). Decentralized approach and involving users/stakeholders as part of the process are never part of project planning. The top-down approach mostly concentrates on long-distance pipelines network for handling the water crisis. The dams, canals and drilling of groundwater which have been the supply side answers to meet the demand are another concern of top-down approach. These concerns of augmenting water supply have not been found sustainable in long-run because of their economic, environmental, ecological, social and human costs. Top-down approach never took cognizance of locally available innovative approaches. The schemes developed in these "Bhavans" are not site specific, neither local people are taken in confidence. The isolated efforts made by people like Rajendra Singh, Magsaysay Award winner who brought a change in Rajasthan using simple traditional approaches of water harvesting with people's involvement are examples to be replicated. The need is for such people and site specific committed group to be involved in addressing water-related issues. Another example is of Dwarka in Gujarat which is a rain deficient area. A traditional approach i.e. rainwater harvesting at household level has solved the acute drinking water problem of the area. On the contrary, there is Cherapunjee in Meghalaya in India, an area of highest rainfall in the country, suffers from an acute shortage of drinking water because it lets rainwater to drain away. Which approach do we want, top-down approach which mostly believes in mega projects or site-specific traditional approach like rainwater harvesting? The country has to decide and act. The solution lies in conserving water where it falls.

Vote Bank Politics in Launching the Schemes

Innumerable schemes covering A to Z of water-related issues are mostly confined on papers but in reality their impacts are rarely visible. Many schemes are announced before election. About 2 decades back, election promise was 'Roti, Kapra, Makan' which was later changed to Bijli, Sadak, Pani. Now we are talking of Shiksha, Swasthya, Suraksha. We have not solved either of the problem so far. Where have these slogans gone? The slogans remain as slogans as part of election manifesto of political parties to attract votes since Independence. Announcing programmes mostly during election, assuring for their execution after the election is won and dropping the schemes on failure and blaming each other have become the culture of people in power in our country. Water is an essential element for life. Any programme or announcement on water before election should not be of temporary nature to simply attract vote to occupy the chair and then forget the promise and befool the people. It is the biggest mockery of our democratic system. How serious are we to address the issues is cited through an example. Israel, a desert country more than Rajasthan is all green now. What is that technology? Scores of people like scientists, agriculturists, planners, politicians and many others' a few more than once visited Israel to see the technology. No efforts have been made to replicate the Israeli technology in India. What did they do there? Did they go on picnic?

Poor and Misleading Database

Information base of this priority area is quite confusing and contradictory. Sometimes you come across strange and contradictory report. Many a times data is presented to suit political and administrative expediency. False and misleading data to please the boss is doing much harm to the system. Most of the time data is made complex and misleading to hide the corrupt practices in the system. Corrupt people take maximum benefit from such data. The country leads in corrupt practices in the world is a known fact. Of the total development assistance only 12 per cent reaches to the end users.

11
Water Management

Water management is a complex process. To understand water management, it is better to understand first 'what is water' and 'who owns it'? Water is a precious natural resource, people collectively own it and how do individuals use this resource without causing damage to the collective need is water management. Climatic conditions and ecology affect water management. Water management in tropical and temperate countries differs in terms of irrigation requirement, flood and drought occurrence, water resource alternatives like dam construction, groundwater recharge, water storage and need for rainwater harvesting. The solutions are site specific and context specific. Many solutions that worked well in the West, may have disastrous results in India.

Understanding of hydrological cycle that mostly depends on sun is important for efficient water management. Heat removes 875 cubic kilometers of water from oceans and 160 cubic kilometers from land surface everyday by evaporation. Evaporation puts water in the atmosphere. Precipitation brings back the total evaporated water to the land. Fresh water available to us is determined by the difference between evaporation and precipitation. This difference is called run-off. The process of water management plan depends on how much of run-off is harvested, stored and used efficiently.

There have been major global shifts in approaches to water management. The first two decades (1950s and 1960s) saw increasing reliance on infrastructure development. The main concentration on subsequent decades was on corporatisation. Water departments were turned into separate State-owned water companies and boards. The tap water in homes was considered indispensable and a status symbol. With such developments, communities alienated from local water and cease to own traditional water systems. The shared responsibility to protect the natural water resource was vanished. The traditional systems have fallen into disuse or disrepair. The major funds were allocated to mega projects like dam construction with little emphasis on maintenance of traditional water resources like rivers, canals, ponds, lakes and tanks. Long-term negligence of traditional system of water conservation led country to suffer from frequent droughts and floods and allowing two-third of water to flow into sea. Launching expensive schemes to build dams and linking rivers to increase supplies are wrong decisions. Even simpler measures to prevent water loss through leakage and theft may prove much effective to improve water supplies. In nearly all the mega cities 40 to 60 per cent of water never reaches the consumer because of leaks and poor maintenance.

The water pollution due to contamination of waterways and undergroundwater by untreated sewage and waste water discharge add to the problem. Decrease in river basin area and decline in water table are also results of poor water management. Even basic knowledge regarding orientation of ponds to store and conserve water efficiently and protecting them from possible damage as specified in 'Vraht Sanhita' during 550 AD have been forgotten in maintaining the ponds. Is it the management, the people of the country expect from the Government? The guidelines regarding orientation of ponds to store and conserve water are: (1) A pond laid East to West retains water for a long time as compared to one from North to South that gets spoiled invariably by waves raised by the winds. (2) Tank walls should be lined with timber or stone for stability. (3) Banks must be shaded with useful trees. (4) An outlet laid with stone should be made on a side for water exit.

WATERSHED MANAGEMENT

Watershed is the basic unit of development involving a manageable hydrological approach. A watershed may be plain, hillock, hill or mountain. Each and every water and land area is a part of one or the other watershed. A watershed may be micro watershed, watershed, catchment and river basin in order of increasing size. The smallest watershed in context of agricultural hydrology may be the field or plot. Watershed management is not simply water harvesting and water conservation but is a multi-objective and multi–sectoral development programme. The approach is integrated and aim is to achieve overall development of the area through soil and water management, agriculture and agroforestry development, improvement in health and education level, rural energy management and community development. The main emphasis of watershed management is on *in situ* moisture conservation where each drop from nature needs to be conserved and used in the most efficient, befitting and cost-efficient manner to sustain agricultural production.

Watershed development in Hill Areas

Watershed development in hill areas covers treatment of entire catchment area with the ridge-to-valley approach. The water is conserved right from the source, i.e., rainwater falling on the hills through various civil structures like contour bunds, graded trenches, bench terraces, gully plugs, check dams and percolation tanks including afforestation. These devices not only conserve the water but also protect the precious top soil from getting eroded due to the stream/rainwater run-off. Planting of soil binding and texture improving grass species and drought resistant tree species along the farm bunds and block planting in waste lands prevent soil erosion and water run-off. To protect the forest area from livestock, either fodder development for stall feeding of livestock and/or rotational grazing should be practised. These devices on steep slopes (35-23%) are effective in checking soil erosion and retaining 80-100 per cent of annual rainfall (2300 mm/annum) *in situ*.

Watershed Development in Rainfed Areas

Watershed development in rainfed areas is more relevant. The green revolution technologies and their benefit are mainly restricted to irrigated agriculture. The gains of green revolution technologies could not sustain and have shown a declining trend and there has been a negative growth for few years during last decade. Rainfed area which constitutes nearly 60 per cent (85 Mha out of 142 Mha total cultivated area) of the net arable area in the country is characterized by low levels of productivity. In order to sustain the growth and obtain higher rate of growth in agricultural sector, it is essential to enhance productivity in rainfed areas. The major impact of watershed development in rainfed areas is to conserve natural resources. The annual soil loss in India is estimated to be about 16.3 tonnes/ha which is mainly due to erosion by water and wind. Rain contributes to over 60 per cent of the loss. Therefore, management of rainwater becomes the key in watershed development in rainfed areas.

Watershed Development Programmes

The concept of watershed development was launched in 1983 with 47 model watersheds in the country. Such a project for the hills was implemented in the State of Punjab, Haryana, Himachal Pradesh and Jammu & Kashmir with an objective to reverse the environmental degradation of the Himalayan foothills through appropriate soil and water conservation technologies. Another project on Integrated Watershed Development for the Plains was implemented in Gujarat, Orissa and Rajasthan to introduce sustainable land management practices in selected watersheds through cost-effective and replicable conservation technologies (vegetative, soil and moisture conservation measures). The pilot projects for watershed development in rainfed areas were implemented in Andhra Pradesh, Karnataka, Maharashtra and Madhya Pradesh from 1983 to 1993 with the objectives: (1) To develop suitable technologies for increasing and stabilizing crop and forage yields, fuelwood and timber in selected rainfed farming areas and (2) To define technical criteria, administrative procedures and investment limits useful in replicating the activities in other areas.

Dozens of programmes are implemented by different Ministries/Departments/Agencies in the countries, *viz.*, National Watershed Development Project for Rainfed Areas (NWDPRA). Soil Conservation for Enhancing Productivity of Degraded Lands in the Catchments of River Valley Projects and Flood Prone Rivers (RVP & FPR), Watershed Development Project in Shifting Cultivation Areas (WDPCA) and Watershed Development Fund under the Ministry of Agriculture; Desert Development Programme (DDP), Drought Prone Area Programme (DPAP) and Integrated Watershed Development Programme under the Ministry of Rural Development; National Afforestation Programme under the Ministry of Environment and Forestry; Hill Area Development Programme (HADP) and Western Ghat Development Programme under the Planning Commission including several Externally Aided Projects. More than a thousand crore is invested annually on watershed development projects in the country. Ministry of Agriculture subsumed all the watershed programmes under macro-management mode of funding in Xth plan. Further a Perspective Plan covering 20 years (2002 to 2022) for treatment of 88 million hectares with an outlay of Rs. 72,750 crore on sharing basis (Centre, State and beneficiaries) was proposed by Planning Commission. Sustainability of programmes and its impact on productivity continues to be a serious concern for long. A major challenge in the execution of watershed programmes is lack of participatory approach. Involvement of several Ministries/departments/agencies adds confusion and conflicts that result in poor delivery.

Impact of Watershed Programmes

- Decline in land degradation through various core activities *viz.*, land development and soil conservation, afforestation, sand dune stabilization, water resources development, integrated watershed development, rainwater harvesting/conservation, fuelwood plantation, recovery of degraded forests, pasture development and roadside plantation.

- Increase in crop productivity and internal rate of return in area covered with watershed programme.
- Other benefits accrued in project area are amelioration of environment, protection of crop land and communication lines from sand dunes, reduction in human drudgery in fetching water from distances.
- Increase in off-season tillage and contour cultivation due to increase in *in situ* rainwater conservation, improved biotypes of crops, soil fertility management and weed control helped in getting optimum production.
- Improvement in rainfed agriculture due to improved rainwater conservation and agronomic practices.
- Diversification by introducing cash yielding oilseed crops in place of less remunerative coarse cereals.
- Improvement in cropped area and cropping intensity and a concomitant rise in number of working days.
- Increase in productivity on a sustainable basis and to improve the quality of life of rural population.

Lessons Learnt from Watershed Programmes in the Country

- The size of the project should be manageable.
- Project should be designed keeping in view the ecology, local indigenous knowledge and priorities of the area. Involvement of farmers is important.
- Participation of beneficiaries, right from identification to implementation of the projects is of paramount importance in watershed management efforts. Benefits to be shared proportionate to contribution.
- Clear demarcation and management of common property resources (such as forest areas or grazing land) is important as it involves changes in legal and policy rules and regulations.

- The sustainability of programmes was questionable since no one owned the responsibility to maintain continuity after the project was completed.
- The successful replicability of results of pilot projects in any watershed was difficult without any Government/ external support.
- Several programmes with similar activities on watershed management simultaneously running in the states, with little coordination and linkages, result in confusion with poor outcome.
- Concentration should be on production-oriented and income-generating activities.
- Community-based approach and developing an institutional mechanism, involving Panchayati Raj Institutions and local communities are important for long-term sustainability.

Guiding Principle of Watershed Management for Sustainable Gains: Guiding principles of watershed management for long-term gains are mentioned below:

Reducing Impact Velocity of Rain Drops: Direct fall of rain drops on exposed earth surface disturbs the soil texture and is the main cause of soil erosion particularly in waste land. Impact velocity can be reduced by establishing vegetation *viz.*, tree cover, grass cover and control on livestock grazing on the soil surface. The practice will prevent soil erosion.

In situ Water Conservation Approach: The *in situ* water conservation measures like contour plough, contour cultivation, contour bunding, recharge trenches, farm pond, silvipasture and afforestation convert the surface flow into sub-surface flow. The practice minimizes displacement of soil, increases soil moisture content of field, groundwater table and groundwater storage.

Water Harvesting in Streams: Run-off if not impounded by mechanical measures emerge as streams. Stream water if not used locally joins rivers or oceans. Live checkdam, store bund, gabion structure, underground *bhandars* are measures to slow down the flow velocity of water and enhances water infiltration.

Adoption of Ridge to Valley Approach: All components of a watershed, i.e. arable land, non-arable land and drainage line are treated as an geo-hydrological entity from ridge to valley.

Integrated Farming System Approach: Integrated farming system approach including diversification as per ecology and farmers' resources provide additional income and long-term sustainability.

People's Participation: Participation of people is utmost important for the success of programme. Community-based approach involving local people who have clear understanding of protecting their resources and a good knowledge of indigenous practices must be adopted.

Institutional Development for Watershed Management: Site specific project development, time-based activity schedule (work plan), its implementation, timely monitoring and evaluation and post-project work plan are important for the success of the project. Watershed development corpus fund should be generated for maintenance of the assets and continuance of activities after the project is over. A provision of revolving fund as income-generating activities for landless farmers should be made.

Post-project Sustainability: Post-project sustainability of watershed programmes continues to be major concern. The reasons are many: (1) Not developing post-project sustainability plan mechanism in most of the projects, (2) Abrupt withdrawal of resources and people's participation soon after the completion of project and (3) An institutional mechanism at village level is not created. These shortcomings should be resolved for long-term sustainability.

WATER MANAGEMENT IN AGRICULTURE

The agricultural sector continues to utilize a lion's share of water resources. Water, agriculture and food security are inter-related. Sustainable agriculture and food security will not be possible without efficient and economic water management. It requires a planned water management strategies, innovative technologies and an institutional arrangement for both irrigated and rainfed agriculture. The efforts should be to produce more food for rapidly growing population by using efficient technologies. About 70 to 80 per cent of the total water consumed is lost mainly because there is no metering of water as a result farmers overextract the groundwater and flood the fields. Flooding damage the soil fertility, declines groundwater level and in long-run, decreases agricultural productivity. Water use efficient approaches are given below:

Multiple Use of Water

Most of the time, water supply systems are designed for a single use. Such systems are often unable to cope with additional demands. Multiple use water systems which are economical in long-run should be introduced. Diverse water sources including waste water use should be explored.

De-silting and Maintenance of Rivers, Canals and Irrigation Channels

Poor maintenance of irrigation channels including water pipes has compounded the problem of water for agriculture. Only 30-40 per cent of water pumped into the canals reach the fields. Desilting and timely repair of rivers and canals improve the water supply.

Free/Subsidized Electricity for Irrigation is Dangerous

Free or subsidized electricity for irrigation not only results huge loss to Government exchequer, i.e. about 24,000 crore per year but also leads to overextraction of groundwater that results in decline in water level and soil salinity problems. There is a need for dialogue between Government and consumer to develop a balance in groundwater extraction and its discharge. There is need for withdrawing free or subsidized electricity and funds saved by withdrawing subsidy be used for developing water conservation technologies. Conventional water resources should be revived to minimize wastage.

Improving Communication and Collaboration among Water Users

Water is often a source of conflict between upstream and downstream users. There is a need for developing dialogue among stakeholders to make them to understand interconnected needs for efficient and equitable water allocations.

Water and Crop Planning

There should be a policy for crop planning as per water availability and ecological situations. Cultivating non-water intensive crops like oilseeds and maize in water deficient areas is advisable. The expansion of paddy cultivation in Punjab and sugarcane in Maharashtra which has led to depletion of groundwater was not a wise planning. Water and electricity being free, people in both the States went for indiscriminate and irrational use of water. Adverse impact on agricultural productivity and soil fertility with excessive use of water is visible. Rice Intensification technology (SRI) which requires less quantity of seed, less nursery area, saves water and labour and enhances yield should be popularized. Aerobic and upland rice technologies should be expended. Crop diversification with high value crops that require less water should be practiced.

Micro-Irrigation Technologies

Drip and sprinkler irrigation instead of flood irrigation should be popularized. Drip and sprinkler irrigation in particular is important for farming on slopes to regulate right amount of water supply to each plant. Pitcher and bamboo systems are other micro-irrigation approaches. The practice of using pitcher water for irrigating fruit plants in areas of scanty rainfall is prevalent in temperate districts of Himachal Pradesh. The pitcher filled with water can maintain moisture for at least 2 weeks. Bamboo channels with small holes made at the inter nodes of open bamboo channels is common practice of irrigation in north–east region of the country. The case of Israel turning desert area into green using drip irrigation systems and other soil and water conservation approaches is before us. When Israel, a much smaller country with more desert area and meagre rainfall can do miracle, why not India?

Moisture Conservation through Mulching

Covering the soil surface with grass or other organic matter is a common mulching practice to conserve soil moisture in the field. The technique is simple and cost-effective.

Water Management in Hills

In spite of high rainfall and origin of several rivers and their tributaries, water has been a scarce commodity in hills to meet the needs of irrigation, drinking and other domestic uses. Most of the agricultural and horticultural production in hills depends on rains. Because of sloppy area and rains being erratic, a high percentage of rainwater goes as run-off and stream flow leaving hardly any water on hills. Therefore, available (rain) water should be conserved properly for dry periods. The scope of bore wells, tube wells, canals and even lift irrigation in hills is limited. The common sources of water to meet irrigation, domestic and drinking needs are small water channels (*Kuhls*), streams and springs, farm ponds, depression and other dugout structures. In cold deserts, the source of water for irrigation and drinking water are perennial torrents, melting snow on the high peaks which comes down as *kuhls* (water channels), streams and springs at certain points. Pand (spang) grass is used for controlling seepage and side losses in water tanks. Harvesting of dew and fog water after the receding of monsoon and their fall on soil surface makes the layer moist and wet.

Wastewater Use in Agriculture

Irrigation with wastewater for cultivation of crops like vegetables, flowers and fodder is a way of life in and around urban areas. Increasing population, urbanization and industrialization and change in lifestyle are expected to produce more wastewater. The main sources of wastewater are domestic and industrial effluents. About 25,000 MLD of domestic wastewater (sewage) and 90,000 MLD of industrial wastewater is generated daily. This amount of wastewater which is very rich in nutrients (N, P and organic matter) is sufficient to irrigate about 1.5 Mha land in the country. Peri - urban agriculture depends largely on wastewater which provides about one million tonnes of nutrients for the cash crops and 130 million mandays of employment to support livelihoods of millions of small landholding farm families.

The present wastewater irrigation practices are primitive, unscientific and more of disposal oriented. Their consistent use results in progressive and irreversible accumulation of salts, toxic chemicals, heavy metals in soil, surface and groundwater that ultimately leads to health and environmental hazards, through a chain: sewage-soil-vegetables-animal-human being. Management of wastewater is a great challenge and opportunity. Sewage water is considered an opportunity particularly for peri-urban agriculture because of its high biodegradable constituents having rich manurial value. Elimination of toxic chemicals, heavy metals and pathogens from the wastewater is, however, a big challenge. Discharge of domestic, industrial and storm water into the same system confounds the use of wastewater. Since the quality aspects of wastewater use in agriculture are related to three main aspects, *viz.*, human and animal health, soil health and optimum crop production, it is imperative to develop proper guidelines for safe utilization of wastewater. The uncontrolled use of waste-water also has serious environmental and health implications. Therefore, policies to cut down water contamination at Government level and a set of guiding principles to minimize the risks at farmers' level should be followed.

Policies on Wastewater Management at Government Level

1. Proper implementation of laws that prohibit mixing of industrial effluents with sewage water.

2. The use of aquatic macrophytes for the removal of toxic pollutants.
3. Investments on R&D to develop cheaper sewage treatment technologies.
4. Incorporating treatment and use of wastewater plan during physical planning of cities.
5. Establishment of wastewater treatment plant by the industries should be made mandatory.
6. Industries allowing their effluents in the drains without treatment should be penalized.

Risk Management Strategies at Farmers' Level

1. The vegetables which are eaten raw should not be cultivated.
2. High value crops like flowers, aromatic grasses and industrial crops should be grown.
3. Drip irrigation, adopting ridge-furrow technique should be emphasized.
4. The contact with wastewater during irrigation and other cultural operations should be minimized. Wearing gumboots, gloves or washing hands and legs with soap after each farming operations are healthy practices.
5. Use of wastewater in public parks, avenue trees and for creating green belts around cities should be promoted.
6. Vegetables should be thoroughly washed before cooking to minimize the contamination.

DAMS AND THEIR RELEVANCE AS WATER STORAGE STRUCTURES

No doubt, the dams form an important part of development process and contributes to irrigation and power generation. It is good so far as progressive famers and urban elites are concerned. But what about the poor farmers and the people who are least benefited and fall in death knell due to displacement and deprivation of their livelihood means. Such mega projects should also be looked in terms of how many villages are submerged and how much area under forests is destroyed.

There is long debate on the efficacy of big dams. Proponents support and justify their construction. The construction of Narmada dam was justified because on completion, the dam would irrigate 2 million hectares of land, supply drinking water to 30 million people, recharge groundwater, combat excess fluoride and generate electricity. Similarly, construction of Tehri dam was justified due to following expected benefits on completion: (1) will provide 2,400 MW power to nine States in North India, (2) annual energy availability would be 3,568 million units of the Northern Grid, (3) would irrigate 2.7 lakh hectares of agricultural land in Uttar Pradesh besides stabilizing irrigation in another 6.4 lakh hectares and (4) would provide 162 MGD drinking water to Delhi and 108 MGD to neighbouring state. The intensively irrigated tracts created by large dams provided food security to the starving country is an established fact but it could not be sustained for long. On the contrary, the opponents of the dam construction warn that the harm caused to the society and environment outweighs its advantages. The opponent's views against dam construction are highlighted below:

1. Dams are not sustainable in long-run to address water problem because life of dams is 30-40 years due to accumulation of silt and melting of glaciers because of global warming will lead to reduction in water flow in rivers and therefore interrupting water supply to dam.
2. Dams destroy habitats, cut rivers off from their flood plains and threaten fish population which is the life support for hundreds of thousand of communities world-wide.
3. Dam construction hinders purification of water in river in two ways: (1) In hills the river after striking with stones cleans water and (2) with change of ecology due to construction of dams, several fish species which clean the water are gradually diminishing.

4. The large dams whether built for irrigation, power or water supply or flood control have adverse ecological impacts and contribute to displacement.
5. The dams that have more water stored than required at the monsoon onset if not managed in time may result in great floods and damages.
6. Large dams in tropical climate are significant source of global warming gases. It may be around 33.5 million tonnes of methane emissions in a year which is responsible for about one-fifth of the country's total global warming impact. Of all the dams in the world, the dams in India produce largest amounts of methane. Hence the notion that dams provide clean power is a myth.

Sustainability of Dams

Most of the dams were built to improve agricultural productivity by augmenting water and power supply. Short-term gains of most of the dams have been significant. But issues related to long-term gains have rarely been debated. A few dams and their long-term impact have been highlighted below.

Bhakra Nangal dam was an era of green revolution for 2-3 decades but has now proved a classic example of long-term catastrophe in Punjab. The startling finding was that Bhakra did not add any new area under irrigation.

The idea of Tehri dam located on confluence of Bhagirathi and Bhilangana rivers was conceived as early as 1949 for sugarcane growers in Western U.P. and to meet the drinking water needs of Delhi. One of the target of this project was to produce 2,400 MW of power. But in the process to achieve these targets, the dam has uprooted over 14,000 families from old Tehri and more than 100 surrounding villages. Moreover, the dam being located in a seismic fault zone is prone for earthquakes. It would be a catastrophe if the dam collapses due to earthquake or any other fault.

The Hirakund dam celebrated its golden jubilee in 2007 at the cost of manyfold tragedies. When dam was built in 1957:

(1) 26,501 families in 249 villages were displaced, (2) 1.83 lakh acres including 1.23 lakh acres of irrigated land submerged in the reservoir and (3) 50,000 people without land were forcibly evicted. Tribals were worst sufferers of dam construction.

Sardar Sarover Project (SSP) has been India's most controversial dam project. The foundation stone of this project was laid in 1961. The work on main SSP began in 1987. Further, work to raise dam's height from 111 meters to 122 meters was taken in 2006. Medha Patkar, a renowned environmentalist and social worker sit on fast on April 5, 2006 to protest for any further increase in Narmada Dam's height. Raising the dam's height by 11 meters will render another 1,50,000 people homeless.

Dam construction is not a passport to enhance water availability, neither free from environmental hazards. A series of dams constructed in Maharashtra to augment water availability for sugar cultivation could not be sustained for long rather left farmer in Maharashtra with acute shortage of water. Indiscriminate dam construction diverting sea bound water to inland use may also result in sea ingress and therefore impacting coastal communities and fishermen in long-run. The decision to construct two dams: one 381 MW Bhairon Ghati and second 480 MW Pala-Maneri hydro-electric plants was dropped in March, 2010 because 55 km area from Gaumukh to Laharinag-Pala being sensitive. Questions have been raised for usefulness of dams in long-run. USA removed 100 dams between 1999 and 2002 and spent billions of dollars to restore rivers by removing dams and embankments.

Social and Economic Aspects of Big Dams

There is long debate in the country on construction of big versus small dams. The issues related to social, equity and sustainability remain unaddressed in large irrigation systems built around big dams. The farmers in the hill and mountain regions who are mostly poor and constitute large part of land area are least benefited with big dams. Building of dams is not cost-effective. The country would have spent more than

Rs. 1,00,000 crore on dams building after Independence. Had we invested even half of this amount in rainwater harvesting and other sustainable alternatives instead of building dams, the things would have been different.

The real long-term solution lies in a decentralized water conservation network along with optimum utilization of the available rainwater resources. A truly decentralized scheme if designed and implemented by a community-based on its needs, using largely its own resources may ensure safe and adequate water supply to rural and urban communities to meet human, agricultural and animal needs.

The idea of doing big tasks for the sake of showing that we are doing big things is not good. Small is beautiful. Small irrigation projects, small power plants and small industries covering wider areas of the country suits to our social fabric. Small projects are safe, can avoid national upsets, rehabilitation problems and many other things associated with big projects. Nehru who once celebrated big dams as the temples of modern India started contemplating more democratic and more scientific alternatives. He realized that a project, big or small should be viewed in terms of its long-term social, economic and environmental perspectives. Too much playing with nature is dangerous. Nature did not like building a big network of canals in Harappa's time. 'Conserving water where it falls' is the approach for long-term sustainability.

FLOODS AND DROUGHTS ARE RESULTS OF MISMANAGEMENT OF WATER RESOURCES

Floods and droughts, simply considered as natural calamities are not correct. More than that these disasters are results of faulty policy and poor management of water resources. Why are many regions of the country going for recurrent droughts when country has highest rainfall in the world? Where has all the rainwater gone? The reasons are not shortage of water. The collapse of traditional systems of rainwater harvesting is the core of the problem. Skewed priorities, poor land and water management, increasingly barren land due to deforestation and uncontrolled grazing by animals, silting of water tanks and canals that allow rainwater to run rather than percolate slowly into the ground and recharge wells and tanks are essentially reasons of droughts. The resources including money which should have gone in preventing deforestation, siltation and other forms of land and water management. Siphoning of money into mega schemes on big dams and canal networks have not delivered results in proportion to money spent on them.

Recurrence of floods is worst than droughts. Crumbling and improper maintenance of drains, illegal river side construction and lack of coordination between engineering, sanitation and water supply departments are main reasons of floods in the monsoon. Sewage and solid wastes that are dumped in natural drains particularly in urban area add to the problem. The situation in metros is worst. Floods in urban areas are more of poor planning and water management. Three major metros - Mumbai, Bangalore and Chennai were under neck deep water in 2005. Poor drainage immobilized these cities for weeks, cause diarrhoea, deaths and economic ruins. Floods in dried districts like Jaisalmer and Barmer, killing more than 150 people in 2006 speaks of volume about poor planning and water management in our country.

12

Strategies for Sustainable Water Development

The whole country is loaded with challenges in the water sector in terms of water availability, overexploitation of groundwater resulting in lowering of groundwater table, vanishing of water bodies, faulty embankment policy, poor addressal of natural disasters like flood and drought, deterioration in water quality, cost and time over-runs in the completion of projects including poor maintenance of infrastructures in spite of spending lakhs of crores of rupees in innumerable schemes on water management. We simply talk of water conservation, judicious use of water and recycling techniques on paper but we never practice. The present water crisis is our own creation. According to an estimate, we use more than three times the quantity of water than is actually required. Delhi may become a city of acute water scarcity if water related issues are not addressed in a focussed manner. Our policies and strategies should now focus on sustainable development and quality improvement of water resources. Rainwater harvesting, groundwater recharge, judicious use of water, avoiding water waste and recycling of wastewater are important strategies to address the water crisis. There is a need for participatory approach to capture and use available water resources efficiently. The ultimate aim is to have adequate water for clean, green and healthy living. For that, country has to revert back to natural process of water harvesting, water conservation and recharge of groundwater. The future of the planet depends on the decisions we take now and implement them expeditiously.

If there is no change in our pattern of consumption, wastage, polluting water resources including our lifestyle, the day is not far off when this planet will become a dustbowl. A beginning has to be made at the earliest. We must be serious to conserve and use water judiciously like our forefathers did in ancient times. The 'Mantra' to solve all water related problems lies in developing a system to harvest, conserve and store primary source of water resources. There is need for passionate, determined and holistic approach on a strict time line as mentioned below.

Protecting Water Bodies and Groundwater Depletion

Mega schemes like building dams or link rivers in a bid to increase water supplies have been the utter failure. The solution lies in indigenous technologies of conserving primary source of water resources for replenishing water bodies to recharge aquifers.

Water Bodies

Water bodies have multiple use. These bodies recharge aquifers, provide habitats for indigenous and migratory birds, help stem food erosion and also serve as eco-tourism spots. Drying of water bodies deprive animals that depend on water bodies for drinking. Encroachments, piling of garbage and sewage entry in water bodies are main challenges confronting the country. Fencing, installing sewage trapping mechanism, grow plants around them and prevent encroachments are certain measures to save water bodies. Framing of rules are vital to stop the life sapping influx of sewage, industrial waste, pesticides, construction debris and other solid wastes into these fragile sites. The protection of water bodies demands a policy framework to make polluters, encroachers including agencies who flout the rule, liable for penalties. The approaches like removal of weeds, silt and other garbage are equally important. Involvement of local people especially the older generation who are emotionally and socially connected in the maintenance and upkeep of water bodies is important. No residential *pattas* should be given on land meant for water bodies. Supreme Court judgement to protect water bodies from encroachments and pollution should be honoured.

Groundwater Recharge

Groundwater level due to overextraction is depleting fast. Blanket ban on groundwater extraction is not rational approach till optimal water availability through other water resources is ensured. Till then only solution to control groundwater extraction is to tax on water extracted groundwater. The electricity for running the bore wells should not be subsidized or free.

Increasing Water Use Efficiency and Reducing Wastage

There is a need to improve water use efficiency to meet the increasing demand from all sectors due to changing lifestyle, urbanization, industrialization and increasing food needs of more mouths over the year. Industries may play a proactive role in managing water. The industry and consumer both must drive the change. While industry would produce water saving devices, the consumers must install them. Empowered Water Bodies could be formed to manage distribution better, cracking down on theft and reducing wastage by replacing leaking pipes by installing hydraulic device in the pipelines/water supply network. Hydraulic Model is vital to 24 × 7 water supply and requires constant monitoring of pressure in the water system to prevent leakages.

Promoting Water Use Efficient Technologies in Agriculture

Agriculture being bulk user of water, water use efficient technologies may be of immense help to save huge amount of water in agriculture. A few proven technologies are mentioned here: (1) multiple use of water, (2) de-silting and maintenance of rivers, canals and irrigation channels, (3) stopping free/

subsidized electricity for irrigation purpose, (4) improving communication and collaboration among water users, (5) crop planning as per water availability and ecological situations, (6) popularizing micro-irrigation technologies (drip and sprinkler irrigation) and (7) practicing mulching to conserve moisture.

Policy to Manage Water in Hills

In spite of high rainfall and origin of several rivers and their tributaries, water has been a scarce commodity in hills to meet the needs of irrigation, drinking and other domestic uses. Most of the agricultural and horticultural production in hills depends on rains. Because of sloppy area and rains being erratic, a high percentage of rainwater goes as run-off and stream flow leaving hardly any water on hills. Therefore, available (rain) water should be conserved properly for dry periods. The scope of bore wells, tube wells, canals and even lift irrigation in hills is limited. The common sources of water to meet irrigation, domestic and drinking needs are small water channels (*kuhls*), streams and springs, farm ponds, depression and other dugout structures. In cold deserts, the source of water for irrigation and drinking water are perennial torrents, melting snow on the high peaks which comes down as *kuhls* (water channels), streams and springs at certain points. Pand (spang) grass is used for controlling seepage and side losses in water tanks. Harvesting of dew and fog water after the receding of monsoon and their fall on soil surface makes the layer moist and wet.

Protecting Water from Pollution

Water borne diseases like cholera, diarrhoea, hepatitis, typhoid, amoebic and bacillary dysentery, hydrated cysts, guinea worms etc. are responsible for heavy toll. Management of waste water which is mostly of domestic, industrial and agricultural origin is important to combat disease incidence. A few policies on wastewater management are highlighted here: (1) Prohibiting mixing of industrial effluents with sewage water, (2) The use of aquatic macrophytes for the removal of toxic pollutants, (3) Developing cheaper sewage treatment technologies, (4) Incorporating treatment and use of wastewater plan during physical planning of cities, (5) Making establishment of wastewater treatment plant by the industries mandatory and (6) Penalizing the industries that allow their effluents in the drains without treatment.

Pricing Water

Free water or very low water tariff in India which is less than 10 per cent of operation cost has resulted in heavy water wastage. Why should water be free? Should it be free because it is a natural resource? The country is spending lakhs of crores of rupees in maintaining water resources and supply infrastructure. Hence, water should have a price to ensure its use more sparingly. However, its cost should be regulated so that poors are not deprived and rich do not waste this natural resource. Rather, incremental slabs should be created in taxing the water supply so that the people who consume more have to pay more.

Public-Private Partnership

The water being a natural resource, it is difficult for public or private sector to work in isolation to address the issues of common interest. There is a need for participatory approach. Public and private sectors both have a role to play. Private sector may be of immense help at introducing innovative ideas, generating financial resources, introducing corporate management, improving service efficiency and accountability. Public sector's main role is coordination and to resolve disputes between the states or with other agencies. Community be empowered and given rights to control the distribution and maintenance of water.

Need for Single Agency to Coordinate Water Related Issues

More than half a dozen agencies/departments/ministries of

Central Government and 35 States including Union Territories claim on water. 'Too many cooks spoil the broth' is proving right to tackle water related issues. There is a need to identify a single agency responsible to coordinate with all the stakeholders and formulate appropriate policies to tackle water related issues. The agency may work on the lines of Singapore's Institute of Water Policy which has been very successful to manage water related issues.

Creating Awareness

Water being fundamental in every area of our life, is to be saved and protected by all means. Domestic cores, irrigation and industries are main consumers of water. Programmes for educating people from all walks of life and creating awareness about importance of water should be organized. Mass awareness campaign through media, lectures, literature, pamphlets and other audio-visual means be organized. Incentives for water harvesting, water conservation and protecting from pollution and any other effort to save water should be created.

Innovative Approaches to Ease the Water Crisis

In country like India which is surrounded by sea on three sides, the sea water after treatment could easily be used for agriculture and other purposes. The treatment of sea water being costly at present, the technology is not in use so far. With recent advancements in membrane technology and possibility of use of alternative energy sources like wind energy, sea currents energy and solar energy, the cost of sea water treatment may go down drastically. The National Institute of Ocean Technology located at Chennai has developed a technology which is simple, cheap and can provide enough water, i.e. one plant commissioned on a boat can make a million litres of sea water fit to drink. In this technology, saline sea water is vapourised and condensed to get potable water.

Innovative approach like condensing the water from air using refrigeration technique is another approach which can be used to make potable water from air. Trials have been made in Jalimudi village in East Godavari district of Andhra Pradesh. Using artificial glaciers to recharge water bodies is another novel water management technique.

Indigenous approaches of water conservation are simple, cost-effective and sustainable in long-run. Two districts (Hubli and Dharwad) of Karnataka made a significant improvement in water supply through indigenous approach. Few hours of water supply is raised to 24 × 7 water supply by (1) deepening and de-silting water reservoirs, (2) replacing rusty iron pipes with leak proof PVC and (3) metering water supply to each residence. Waste was reduced from 30-50 per cent to 5-6 per cent including doubling of tariff collection.

People like Anna Hazare in Maharashtra, Hardev Singh Jadeja in Gujarat, Rajendra Singh in Rajasthan and many others who have shown a way to ease the water crisis through community involvement and participation using traditional wisdom should not be forgotten. There are several cases where people brought back dead rivers, e.g. Rupa, Sarsa and Arvari in Alwar district of Rajasthan to life through community approach using simple traditional wisdom. The country should not forget the traditional wisdom.

STRATEGIC ACTION POINTS

There is a need for participatory approach with active involvement of the Government, NGOs, Private Sector, Panchayati Raj Institutiions and Farmers for sustainable gains. Available resources should be captured and used efficiently for maximum benefits. A sleuth of majors to be taken at individual and at community level are given below:

Communitybased Approach

- Harvesting rainwater from roof tops, from run-offs of local catchments, seasonal flood waters and local streams. Roof top rainwater harvesting should be made mandatory in every house and colony.

- Repair, Renovation and Restoration (RRR) of water bodies. The water bodies should be cleared of encroachments.
- Planting canopy of trees on both sides of the road and keeping central verge (of about 1 meter width) of road *kachcha* for improving groundwater percolation.
- Installing a hydraulic model, a satellite map of the pipelines for constant monitoring of pressure in the water system to prevent leakage.
- Providing sewer lines in all the colonies to stop untreated sewage flow directly into the river.
- Recycling of residential waste water through water treatment plants. Installation of waste water recycling system in all non-residential buildings having a discharge of 10,000 litres per day should be made mandatory.
- Replacing rusty iron pipes and leaking pipe lines with leak proof PVC pipes and installing meters to record bulk supply and individual consumption.
- Empowering local bodies to manage water distribution.
- Ensure that the water which drains into the water bodies is properly treated before its release.
- Municipal wastes should not be dumped in open. The sewage and industrial effluents should be allowed in rivers and other water bodies only after treatment.
- Introduction of appropriate technology to ensure efficient use of water in the cooling process, controlling pollution, maximizing recycling and reuse. Insist for using water efficient appliances.
- Introduction of drip and sprinkler irrigation for agricultural lands, parks and gardens.
- Make installation of water meter compulsory in each residence. Also introduce competitive water prices, so that those consuming more have to pay more.

- Legal action on misuse of water (illegal tapping, theft, use of water for wrong practices, using potable water for non-domestic purposes and on-line booster).
- Creating mass awareness about importance of water, its conservation and efficient use through *Jal Yatras*, articles, shows on Doordarshan, talks on All India Radio, puppet shows, street plays on specific occasion such as Independence Day, Republic Day, World Water Day etc.
- Demonstrations on rainwater harvesting and artificial recharge to groundwater.
- Organizing art and essay competitions and distribution of booklets, leaflets, folders on water conservation for school/college students.
- Organizing training programmes for Government officials, voluntary agencies and other professionals on water management.
- Imparting timely information to concern agency regarding leakage and bursting of pipelines in the city. Keep watch on use of groundwater particularly by big commercial and industrial users.
- Institution of an annual award for innovative practice on rainwater harvesting and artificial recharge.
- Participatory watershed development and de-silting and renovation of ponds, tanks and reservoirs.
- Settle river water sharing disputes amicably.
- Use of sea water along the coast for raising mangrove and salicornia plantation together with aquaculture.
- Depend more on local sources of water instead of bringing water from far off places at considerable cost. Use water where it drops.
- Catchments should be protected from encroachment at all costs.
- Use improved water conservation practices such as residue management etc.
- Site and ecology specific cropping pattern.
- Promotion of basin level integrated water resources management.

- Conjunctive use of both surface and groundwater.
- Implement participatory irrigation management.

Individual Approach

All of us should save water and use it more sparingly. The responsibility of an individual is not simply to preach sermon about water conservation but to practice religiously. Here are few tips to be observed by each household.

In the Bathroom

- Do not leave the tap running during brushing the teeth, shaving, washing of hands and cloths.
- Judicious use of showers.
- Fill your bath tub only halfway and close it before turning on the water.
- Check water taps, pipelines and toilet tank for leaks. Seal if necessary.
- Internal service pipelines if rusted and corroded should be immediately changed.
- Putting a container filled with water in toilet tank (cistern) can save 1-2 litres of water in each flush or install low flush toilets or switch over to ventilated improved pit latrines (which is odourless and does not use water).
- Ensure that all the taps are closed when not in use. Also ensure repair of dripping faucets.
- Run the washing machine only when full and adjust the water level carefully.

In the Garden/Park

- Trees and shrubs with deep root systems should be watered less frequently than shallow rooted plants which require smaller amounts of water more often.
- Most lawns, shrubs, vegetables and flowers need just one inch of water a week. Do not flood them. Water

them during cool parts of the day to cut down evaporation.

- Use sprinkler and drip irrigation system for watering gardens and lawns. Water small areas of grass/flower pots using bucket rather than hose pipe.
- Plantation during the spring or fall requires less water with high survival rate.
- Use organic manure as it improves water holding capacity of soil and acts as a blanket to keep moisture in and helps prevent erosion, soil compression and weeds.
- Check for and repair of leaky hose connections and sprinkler valves.
- Porous paving materials such as brick, granite or gravel help keep water in the garden.
- Water from kitchen and bathing areas should be recycled, treated and used in garden and parks. Government provides subsidy in establishing recycling mini plant.
- Water your kitchen garden and/or plants during early morning hours to minimize evaporation.

In the Kitchen

- Do not leave the water running while washing the dishes. Better to use two buckets, one for washing and another for rinsing the dishes. Use dishwasher only when full.
- Do not wash vegetables and fruits in running water. Use a small bucket.
- Do not use running water to thaw frozen foods.

Other Water Saving Devices

- Intermittent water supply schedule reduces wastage of water.
- Do not use drinking water to clean car and for moping floor.

- Use water efficient appliances that can save as much as 35 per cent water.
- Do not use running hose pipe for washing floor and car.
- A simple strainer in the wash basin will reduce overflow of water by 50 per cent.
- Do not put water down the drain. Such water may be used for watering the plants or for cleaning.
- Use a broom instead of hose pipe to clean common places.

13
Summary

The water is the most precious natural resource. A person in ancient time used to enjoy special merit in the society who constructed wells, ponds, tanks and other structures. There are many references of wells, canals, tanks, ponds and dams as potential water resources in ancient literature. Even invaders from abroad could understand the wealth of water. India which was one of the wettest countries in the world due to immense reservoirs of water in the form of Himalayas in the North, the Arabian Sea in the West, the Indian Ocean in the South and the Bay of Bengal in the East has become a nation of acute water scarcity during 60 years of Independence. Water availability in the country has come down from 6,500 cubic meters to 2,500 cubic meters per person per annum and will be further reduced to stress level of 1,000 cubic meters per person per annum with growing population, change in lifestyle and cropping pattern, increasing industrialization and urbanization coupled with poor management of water resources. Two-third of rainwater flowing in the sea has made water not only a sparse commodity but also dangerously polluted. Of the total water on earth, only 2.5 per cent is fresh water. Of fresh water about 75.2 per cent lies frozen in polar regions, 22.6 per cent as groundwater and 2.2 per cent is available in lakes, rivers, ponds, atmosphere, moisture, soil and vegetation. Our concern is mainly surface (pond, tanks, lakes, rivers etc.) and groundwater that has been summarized in this chapter.

SURFACE WATER RESOURCES AND THEIR STATUS

The main surface water resources are rivers and canals, tanks and ponds, beels and lakes. The total length of rivers and canals is about 180 thousand km and water bodies cover an area of about 7 mha (of which tanks and ponds have maximum area-2.9 mha followed by reservoirs - 2.1 mha and beels and lakes - 2 mha). Rainwater (precipitation) is primary source of water to feed both surface and groundwater resources.

Water Bodies

Since time immemorial, ponds and other water bodies in the country have been the potential sources of water to meet day to day domestic and other requirements of water. Almost total rainwater was detained in these water bodies. Silting and vanishing of these water bodies have led country from water surplus stage to a water deprivation stage. As a result, not only groundwater table has fast depleted but the quality of both ground and surface water has also deteriorated. Even basic knowledge regarding orientation of ponds to store and conserve water efficiently and protecting them from possible damage as specified in 'Vraht Sanhita' during 550 AD have been forgotten in maintaining the ponds.

There were more than 20 lakh water bodies in the country during Independence. Delhi alone had more than 700 water bodies. Most of the water bodies (big or small) in the country are now heavily silted or used as garbage dumps or are at different level of encroachment. Hardly any attention is being paid to revive or to improve the water bodies, that have multiple uses. These bodies recharge aquifers, provide habitats for indigenous and migratory birds, help stem food erosion and also serve as eco-tourism spots. Drying of water bodies deprives animals that depend on water bodies for drinking water needs.

All water bodies need repair, cleaning and de-silting. Fencing, installing sewage trapping mechanism, growing plants around them and preventing encroachments are certain measures to save water bodies. Framing of rules are vital to stop the life sapping influx of sewage, industrial waste, pesticides, construction debris and other solid wastes into these fragile sites. The protection of water bodies demands a policy framework to make polluters, encroachers including agencies who flout the rule, liable for penalties. The approaches like removal of weeds, silt and other garbage are equally important. Involvement of local people especially the older generation who are emotionally and socially connected in the maintenance and upkeep of water bodies is important. No residential *pattas* should be given on land meant for water bodies. Supreme Count judgment to protect water bodies from encroachments and pollution should be honoured. According to a study if we convert 3 per cent of our land in ponds, country's water crisis will be over. The work is simple, does not require outsourcing of expertise and can be done using local experience in a participatory mode. State Governments with involvement of Gram Panchayats may play a lead role in reviving and restoring the water bodies.

Rivers and Canals

India is a land of many rivers: 14 big rivers, 55 medium rivers and hundreds of small rivers that cover an area of about 329 million hectares. The total river length is approximately 45,000 kilometers catering needs of 80 per cent of the country's population. Encroachments over the years have reduced the river basins and water storage capacity and slowed down their flow. Encroachments, poor maintenance and silting of rivers, canals and irrigation channels have reduced their potential drastically for agriculture. Only 30-40 per cent of water pumped into the canals reach the field. Many rivers are poor vestiges of the past due to their long neglect. Ganga, Yamuna and Sabarmati have lost their ability to assimilate, regenerate and revive and are highly polluted. In Yamuna alone, more than 200 million litres of effluents and sewage are dumped everyday.

Groundwater

Groundwater provides for over 70 per cent of the irrigated area and about 80 per cent of domestic needs. The excessive groundwater drawal in recent past has led to rapidly falling of groundwater level. Over the last 2 decades, as much as 84 per cent of total addition to the net irrigated areas has been groundwater linked.

Precipitation

India's average annual precipitation is about 1,170 mm covering a land area of 3.28 million sq. km. Thus, the volume of annual precipitation comes to 3,840 cubic km. Of total precipitation, about 17.5 per cent water evaporates immediately from the soil, 37.5 per cent flood out into the sea and 20 per cent for various hydrological purposes, leaving only 25 per cent (about 960 cu. km.) water available for different purposes by human beings.

Rain is primary source of water whereas rivers, ponds, tanks, lakes and groundwater are all secondary sources of water. In other words, rain is the ultimate source that feeds all these secondary sources. Ignorance of rainwater harvesting and not storing it for a long time is the main cause of water crisis. In most of the metropolitan cities including Delhi, the loss of rainwater is much higher i.e. about 60 per cent is drained in sea, 30 per cent goes as waste in gutter along with industrial and household sewage and hardly 10 per cent is harvested. Construction of 'Pucca' roads, flats, industrial establishments and Government offices in most of the metropolitans have left very little 'Kachcha' space through which rainwater can percolate into the ground.

DEPLETION OF WATER RESOURCES

We all want water and quality water. We know that we have it but it is not available. We also know where it has gone and how it has gone. Development of tap water has alienated communities from local water and ceased to own traditional water systems. Since the traditional water resources like rivers, canals, ponds, tanks, lakes etc. have fallen into disuse or disrepair and their long-term negligence has led country to suffer from frequent droughts and floods and allowing two-thirds of water to flow into sea. Keeping a blind eye for a long time, we have reached to a state of acute water crisis. It is time to wake up now. There is no use of digging the well when there is fire.

Surface Water Depletion

The country is fast losing its surface water resources. A large number of rivers, streams, canals, ponds and tanks have been either encroached upon or have turned into garbage dumps over past few decades. The people have become insensitive to understand the natural hydrological cycle. Protecting and conserving the surface water bodies are considered no body's concerns. The surface water bodies, mainly around urban villages with little or no sewer facilities, have become the receptacles of the wastes like garbage, sewer and effluents that diminishes their water storage capacity and water quality.

Over the last 200 years, the country has either lost or reduced storage capacity of two million big and small traditional water harvesting resources and wetlands due to poor maintenance, siltation, indiscriminate construction of big concrete dams and other infrastructures. Per capita availability of water that depends in their storage capacity varies greatly between countries. India amongst the semi-arid countries has the lowest capacity to store water. Its per capita storage capacity is 213 cubic meters (m^3) as against 4,733 m^3 in Australia, 1,964 m^3 in the United States and 1,111 m^3 in China. The reservoirs in India can store less than 6 months worth of average flow as compared to reservoirs in the world that can store more than 800 days of average flow. Water storage capacity of rivers is woefully inadequate, barely enough for 30 days of rainfall, compared to 900 days in the major river basins abroad. The area irrigated through tanks and ponds, i.e. non-conventional sources has decreased from 21 per cent in 1958-59 to 6.8 per cent in 1991-92. The need for storage will grow with climate change, variability in rainfall and other extreme events and to meet greater demand of water with population growth, urbanization, industrialization and more area under irrigated agriculture.

Groundwater Depletion

According to Planning Commission Report, 634 Billion Cubic Meters (BCM) is the total water used from underground resources of which 432 BCM is annually replenishable. The rate of extraction of groundwater exceeds the rate of recharge in many parts of the country, i.e. 432 BCM is replenished against 634 BCM extracted from underground resources annually. Delhi is at the top in overextraction (78%), followed by Punjab (75%), Rajasthan (59%), Haryana (49%) and Tamil Nadu and Karnataka both at 37 per cent. Growing of water intensive crops and availability of subsidized or free power in many states nave resulted in overextraction of water for irrigation that consumes about 80 per cent of groundwater resources. Urbanization, industrialization and increased population have put huge pressure on water and to meet it one has to go for overextraction of groundwater. Over-exploitation of groundwater has resulted in lowering of groundwater table, vanishing of water bodies, occurrence of natural disasters like flood and drought including deterioration of water quality. Erratic water supply and poor maintenance of canals have compelled people to go for digging tube wells both for domestic and irrigation purposes. The situation becomes more grave with increase in population and change in lifestyle. About 30 per cent of the country's population are mining much more groundwater than is recharged every year. According to a report from National Aeronautics and Space Authority (NASA), the groundwater level in Northern India (Haryana, Punjab, Rajasthan and Delhi) is disappearing at the alarming rate over the past decade which is faster than natural recharge process. In many places, borings are drying and re-boring is unsuccessful due to fast decline in water table. One-fourth of the country is moving towards deserts, particularly vast areas in U.P, Bengal, Orissa and Maharashtra. Increase in extraction structures (bore wells, tube wells etc.) from 4 million in 1951 to nearly 20 million at present without needed recharge and conservation efforts has resulted in deepening of wells, thereby increasing pumping lifts, investments and energy costs, arsenic toxicity and salinity.

Strategies for Water Conservation

We simply talk of water conservation, judicious use of water and recycling techniques on paper but we never practice. The present water crisis is our own creation. According to an estimate, we use more than three times the quantity of water than is actually required. Delhi may become a city of acute water scarcity if water related issues are not addressed in a focussed manner. Our policies and strategies should now focus on sustainable development and quality improvement of water resources. Rainwater harvesting, groundwater recharge, judicious use of water, avoiding water waste and recycling of waste water are important strategies to address the water crisis. There is a need for participatory approach to capture and use available water resources efficiently. The ultimate aim is to have adequate water for clean, green and healthy living. For that, country has to revert back to natural process of water harvesting, water conservation and recharge of groundwater. The future of the planet depends on the decisions we take now and implement them expeditiously. If there is no change in our pattern of consumption, wastage, polluting water resources including our lifestyle, the day is not far-off when this planet will become a dustbowl. A beginning has to be made at the earliest. We must be serious to conserve and use water judiciously like our forefathers did in ancient times. The 'Mantra' to solve all water related problems lies in developing a system to harvest, conserve and store primary source of water resources. A passionate, determined and holistic approach for sustainable water development on a strict timeline has been described in the book.

14
Action Plan in Project Mode

Why is India, one of the wettest countries in the world with an average precipitation of 1,170 mm that comes to about 400 million hectares of rain and snowfall per annum becoming a nation of acute water scarcity? India receives most of its rainfall in just 100 hours out of the 8,760 hours in a year as compared to western countries where rainfall hours are manyfold. High rainfall in a short span of time results in overflow and drains through rivers in the sea. Long neglect, heavy silting and encroachments have lost water storing capacity of surface water resources in the country.

There is enough water on earth provided we conserve it, store it and use it efficiently. 'Give and Take' is the general rule of life. If you harvest rainwater, store it, recharge groundwater and use it efficiently, it will continue infinitely. "Khet Ka Pani Khet Mein, Gaon ka Pani Gaon Mein" is the basic principle of water conservation. Follow principle of "Use water where it drops', rather than bringing water from far-off places at considerable cost.

We often talk of water crisis at national/international water forum. We blame everything from population growth, urbanization, industrialization, Government and lack of political will but we forget our ancient wisdom of water conservation. The 'Mantra' to solve water related problems lies in reviving our traditional system of harvesting, conserving and storing primary source of water resources. There is need for passionate, determined and holistic approach on a strict timeline and to put an action plan in place for sustainable gains.

Proposed action plan is developed in project mode "National Water Security Mission" and its success depends on how much of run-off is harvested, stored and conserved. For that country has to revert back to natural process of water harvesting, water conservation and recharge of groundwater. Renovation, restoration and maintenance of water bodies like rivers and canals, ponds and tanks, lakes and baolis and other reservoirs are the focus of the project. This will result improving of rainwater harvesting with minimum flow to the sea.

NATIONAL WATER SECURITY MISSION

Background Information and Need for Proposed Project

There have been innumerable schemes/policies on water sector supported by Central and State Governments, World Bank, Asian Development Bank, NGOs and private sector to augment water supply for meeting the agricultural, industrial and drinking water needs of the country. A list is annexed (Annexure-A). A few schemes and their outcomes have been described in detail. The first water policy enumerated by the Government in 1987 and revised in 2002 has remained a policy on paper only. The country has spent billions of rupees on water management in last 60 years. More than an amount of Rs. 1 lakh crore on drinking water schemes and more than 1.4 lakh crore on canal/dam irrigation schemes have been spent by the Government. Estimated outlay for river linking scheme alone at the present cost is about 10 lakh crore if work is done as per plan. In spite of huge expenditure, there has not been any increase in drinking water availability nor the area under canal irrigation has increased. Rather situation is getting bad to worse over the years. India's per capita water availability has declined to one-third in last 60 years and is projected to fall to one-fourth by 2025. Water crisis cannot be overcome by mega and expensive schemes alone.

Most of the programmes run in isolation. One does not know what others are doing. The programmes on drinking waters do not know, what the programmes on irrigation are doing. There is no synergy with each other. Lack of focussed and targeted aims, poor planning, delay in implementation, clash of interest of different agencies involved in the work, no monitoring, evaluation and post-project sustainability plan, no accountability of defaulters, excessive inertia, incompetence, inefficiency, corruption, political interference and wasted interests in the system at all levels are reasons of failure. The issues like participation, incentive, water entitlements, transparency, entry of the private sector, competition, accountability, financing and environmental quality which are not part of the management plan in most of the programmes are other reasons of poor performance or failure of the schemes. Total funds spent on different schemes on water, environment, climate change, pollution, sanitation and several other social and developmental schemes are lakhs of crores of rupees per annum. 90 per cent of the funds allocated in most of the schemes are going in drains due to reasons given above. Need is for a single scheme with clear mandate and is monitored by single agency at central level to address the problem. The proposed scheme, "National Water Security Mission" is an outcome of long failures of water related schemes in the country. The proposed scheme is developed after merging three major schemes: (1) Interlinking of river project (2) National Rural Employment Guarantee Scheme (NREGS) and (3) Member of Parliament Local Area Development (MPLAD) Scheme (Annexure-A)

Rationale

Water crisis is a serious problem and its solution is the national priority. Hundreds of projects/schemes on water related issues in spite of spending lakhs of crores of rupees during last 5-6 decades have been a failure in providing safe water for domestic, agricultural and industrial use. The project under reference is an attempt to override the shortcomings of earlier projects and to work in a missionary zeal with set goals and objectives. The expected outcome to augment fresh water availability within a period of 5 years is assured as per the work plan of the project. Post-project sustainability plan with provision of sustainability fund and an institutional arrangement is built to maintain continuity of gains. The aim is not simply to augment water availability but improving quality of water, employment generation, agricultural productivity, decline in soil erosion, preventing losts of biodiversity, afforestation and improving social and economic status of the people in long-run. Ultimate aim is to make clean, green, healthy and happy India.

Mission

To provide adequate safe water to every person for domestic, agricultural and industrial needs on a sustainable basis.

Aim

To augment fresh water availability, employment opportunities, knowledge empowerment and enrichment of environment and social values in long-run.

Objectives

1. To repair, renovate and revive water bodies like ponds, tanks, lakes etc.
2. To repair, renovate and revive rivers and canals.
3. Watershed management in hill and mountain region.
4. Capacity-building and knowledge empowerment.
5. To develop an institutional mechanism for long-term sustainability.

Features

1. The approach is focussed and targeted.
2. The programme has bottom-up approach rather than top-down.
3. The operational area covers rural, urban, hill and mountain, backward and tribal families.

4. To work in partnership mode—Government, private sector, NGOs and staff on contractual basis (helper, accountant, IT professionals and experts) at village, block, district, state and national level.
5. Enough employment opportunities for poor, landless and unemployed youths from rural, urban and disadvantaged regions.
6. Synergy with development departments, NGOs, civil society organizations, Panchayati Raj Institutions, water user groups to achieve larger, wider and faster impacts.
7. Monitoring and Concurrent Evaluation is integral part of the scheme.
8. The project proposal includes reporting schedule, impact assessment and sustainability plan.
9. Introducing cheque books among job card holders for payment through bank.
10. Two functionaries (one maintaining the muster rolls and second paying the wages) to operate independently to safeguard against embezzlement.
11. Developing information and expert system for water resources and their status.
12. Provision of award for outstanding performance.

Components of the Work

1. To repair, renovate and revive surface water resources on plain and hills.
2. Capacity-building and knowledge empowerment.
3. Developing an institutional mechanism for long-term sustainability.

Repair, Renovate and Revival of Surface Water Resources

The work includes repair, renovate and revival of surface water resources both on plain and hills. The storage capacity of the traditional water harvesting resources and wetlands have been either lost or reduced due to poor maintenance, siltation, indiscriminate construction of dams and other infrastructures. Rain (precipitation) is the primary source of water to feed both surface and groundwater resources which are the secondary sources. Therefore, it is to be harvested and stored and the only way to store this precious primary source of water is through traditional approaches. Conserving rainwater in ponds and tanks and its percolation into groundwater is a cheap and healthy practice of groundwater recharge throughout the country. There are about 20 lakh water bodies covering an area of about 7 mha (of which ponds and tanks have maximum area - 2.9 mha, reservoirs - 2.1 mha and beels and lakes - 2 mha) in the country. Most of these water bodies are heavily silted or used as garbage dumps or are encroached upon for construction and/or agricultural use. These water bodies, big or small once existed anywhere in the country would be cleared of encroachment and repaired, renovated and restored to a level so that water bodies cover at least 3 per cent of land in the country to overcome the water crisis. The work related to repair, renovation and revival of water bodies does not require outsourcing of expertise and can be done using local experience in participatory mode.

India is a land of many rivers; 14 big rivers, 55 medium rivers and hundreds of small rivers that cover an area of about 329 million hectares. The total length of rivers and canals is about 1,80,000 km (river length - 45,000 km and canal length - 1,35,000 km). Encroachment and heavy silting of river beds and canals have reduced their storage capacity and water flow. Desilting and to get rid of encroachment on river basin and canals are the major works in the project.

In spite of high rainfall and origin of several rivers and their tributaries, water has been a scarce commodity in hills to meet the needs of irrigation, drinking and other domestic uses. Most of the agricultural and horticultural production in hills depends on rains. Because of sloppy area and rains being erratic, a high percentage of rainwater goes as run-off and stream flow leaving hardly any water on hills. Therefore, available (rain) water should be conserved properly for dry periods. The scope of bore wells, tube wells, canals and even lift irrigation in hills is limited. The common sources of water to meet irrigation, domestic and drinking needs are small water channels (Kuhls), streams and springs, farm ponds, depression and other dugout structures. In cold deserts, the source of water for irrigation and drinking water are perennial torrents, melting snow on the high peaks which comes down as *kuhls* (water channels), streams and springs at certain points. Watershed development in hill areas that includes treatment of entire catchment area with the ridge-to-valley approach is the way to conserve water right from the source, i.e. rainwater falling on the hills through various civil structures like contour bunds, graded trenches, bench terraces, gully plugs, check dams and percolation tanks including afforestation. These devices not only conserve the water but also protect the precious top soil from getting eroded due to the stream/ rainwater run-off. Planting of soil binding and texture improving grass species and drought resistant tree species along the farm bunds and block planting in waste lands prevent soil erosion and water run-off. To protect the forest area from livestock, either fodder development for stall feeding of livestock and/or rotational grazing are practiced. These device on steep slopes (35-23%) are effective in checking soil erosion and retaining 80-100 per cent of annual rainfall (2300 mm/annum) *in situ*.

Capacity-building and Knowledge Empowerment

Empowering people with knowledge about importance of water, traditional approaches for water harvesting and conservation including repair, renovation and revival of water bodies is important for long-term and sustainable gains. A provision of two types of trainings should be kept in the project: one for project personnel that mostly includes project implementing staff (departmental and contractual staff) and other for beneficiaries/end users. A provision of need-based consultancy to help capacity-building at each project unit should be included in project plan.

An Institutional Mechanism for Long-term Sustainability

Maintenance of river basins and water bodies is not one time task. It demands sustained efforts and hence a need for post-project sustainability plan. Regular dredging and desilting should be taken up in a system mode to improve carrying capacity and flow of the rivers and canals and to improve storage capacity of ponds and tanks. There is need for fencing, installing sewage trapping mechanism, plantation around water bodies and preventing of encroachments. A policy framework to make polluters, encroachers or any other agency who flouts the rules liable for penalties should be developed. The periodical removal of weeds, silt and other garbage is important. Piling of garbage and draining sewer and effluents in and around water bodies should be banned. The involvement of local people especially the older generation who are emotionally connected in the maintenance and upkeep of water bodies is important. No residential *pattas* should be given on land meant for water bodies.

Sustainability Funds

Creation of sustainability funds during the project period is important for maintenance of assets and water resources after completion of the project. Sustainability funds are raised at the rate of 20 per cent of project cost (10% of project cost by State Government and 10% by the beneficiaries) during the project period. The revenue generated by sale of silt (a good fertilizer) and by donations should also be deposited as sustainability fund. The amount received under sustainability fund should be put in fixed deposit account in a bank and to be operated by Sustainability Fund Management Committee located at district headquarters. The funds will be utilized as per contribution made towards each unit (a village) during the project period. The Management Committee may consist of a chairman (Government official), two representatives from the Government, one NGO/private sector and one beneficiary.

The funds will be utilized after the project completion for the common cause and not to serve an individual cause.

Project Formation and Partners

Each village is a basic unit of block plan. The district plan is developed after compiling the block plans. District plans will then be compiled at the state level and finally a plan at national level is developed. The plan is envisaged to cover each and every village of the country. The partners in the project are from top (Nodal Agency) to grass-roots level (water users). The work to each partner is identified according to an agreed work plan and dimension of the work in the area. The partners may be from Central and State Government departments, institutes, universities, private enterprises, voluntary organizations, NGOs, Panchayati Raj Institutions.

Operational Area

The operational area covers each and every village under the 5 Agro-eco regions of the country, i.e. hill and mountain, irrigated, rainfed, arid and coastal areas.

Project Duration and Date of Commencement

The Project is for 5 years and date of sanction is the date of commencement of the project.

Phasing of Project

The project will have roughly 3 phases: (1) an initial phase of six months for pre-project activities that includes base line information on water resources and their status, to analyse the dimension of work and manpower requirement, orientation and sensitization of stakeholders, identification of targets, output and outcome indicators, (2) project implementation *per se* and (3) a final phase of 6-months for post-project activities like report writing, impact assessment and developing post-project sustainability plan for long-term sustainability.

Governance

Project implementation units at national, state, district, block and village level should be constituted to coordinate and oversee the work at different levels. Project implementation units may include relevant line departments, autonomous organizations, Government institutions, research bodies, experts, professionals, panchayat representatives and Voluntary Organizations (VOs). Members of PIUs should have experience of water management and related aspects. Water users association and self-help group concept is more appropriate for the success of the programme. The role of Gram Panchayats is very important and should contribute in following ways: (1) to supervise and support water users associations, (2) to authenticate the accounts/expenditure statements of water users associations and other institution of the project, (3) to maintain the asset register and retain it after the project is over and (4) to provide space/working place and other requirements of water users association. The Ministry of Water Resources, Government of India should be at the top of governance as shown below:

Level of Governance	*Agency*	*Coordinating Officer*
National	Water Resources Department (Govt. of India)	Secretary (Chief Executive Officer)
State	Water Resources Department (State Government)	Secretary (State Coordinator)
District	District Development Office	Jila Parishad Chairman (District Coordinator)
Block	Block Development Office	BDO (Block Coordinator)
Village	Village Panchayat	Sarpanch (Village Coordinator)

Monitoring Mechanism

Concurrent monitoring and evaluation is important for successful implementation and progress of the project. There should be internal and external systems to closely monitor both physical and financial performance in implementation of the programme. The mechanism should also assess the pace and quality of work performed in the project. A web enabled Management Information System (MIS) should be developed. The project website should have project details.

Internal Monitoring

1. A web enabled Management Information System (MIS) should be developed at village level, block level, district level, state level and at national level. It should have checks for ensuring consistency and conformity to normative processes. Informations on all critical parameters like muster rolls, sanctioned works, works under execution, employment provided and financial indicators and wage payment are available on system. 2. Quarterly/half yearly progress report should be developed at district level (merging village-wise reports), state level (merging district-wise reports) and national level (merging state-wise reports).

External Monitoring

It should include statutory institutional mechanism and external reviewers. National Water Security Council (NWSC) constituted at national level and Comptroller Auditor General (CAG) as part of the statutory mechanism to review the project implementation and physical progress at state level: and CAG to audit the project respectively. Review teams constituted at different levels: Central, State, district, block and village should review the project at Central, State, district, block and village level.

Monitoring is based on six monthly report, annual report and workshop, mid-term report and workshop, final report and workshop, monitoring against indicators and impact evaluation against indicators. Monitoring includes the entire results hierarchy. A schematic diagram is given below:

Results Hierarchy

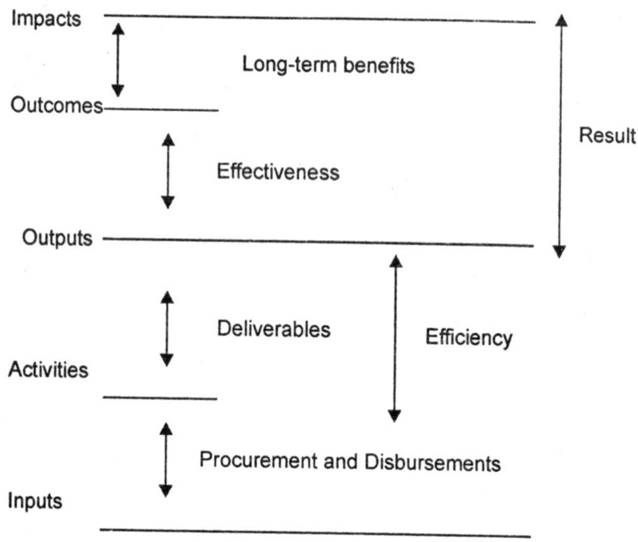

Monitoring and Evaluation in terms of Outlays, Outputs and Outcomes

Outlays are the head-wise/year-wise/centre-wise budget allocations in the project. The total cost of the project and annual expenditure to be linked with outcomes. Outputs are intermediatory stages between outlays and outcomes. Output is the measure of physical progress achieved through an activity under a project. The outcomes are the end products/results of various initiatives and interventions. The outcomes cover the quality and effectiveness of the product achieved through an activity or intervention.

Guiding Principles of M&E Process

1. To ensure that the implementation of activity schedule is as planned.
2. To ensure that the resources are allocated according to the programme.

3. To ensure that the objectives are focussed and achieved in a time frame.
4. To ensure that the Project Implementation Units at different levels are in close coordination and are made responsible for monitoring and evaluation.
5. To ensure that the project evaluation teams at different units have been put in place and funds are released in time.
6. To ensure that the progress is monitored on the basis of measurable indicators at different stages of project implementation.
7. To ensure that the monitorable indicators are developed as per the nature of the project.
8. Data collection process should be objective to the extent possible.
9. Use early/mid-term evaluation results for re-design of the later phases of the project.
10. Evaluation results should be included in the Implementation Completion Report (ICR) and in the final report.

Expected Outcome and Impact

Outcome

- Improvement in water storage, water supply and water quality.
- Assured and sustained water supply.
- Increase in irrigated area.
- Equitable water delivery to all sections of society.
- Reduction in fresh water losses in sea.

Impact

Augmentation of fresh water availability for domestic, agricultural and industrial purposes is the direct impact of the project. Improvement in productivity particularly agricultural productivity, enrichment of environment including reduction in soil degradation, improvement in health and social security with ample opportunity for employment generation, are long-term impacts. A clean, green, healthy and happy India in a span of 5 years will be biggest achievement of the project. Everybody, may be domestic user, agriculturist and an industrialist is a beneficiary.

Budget and Components of Expenditure

The total budget required for 5 years project is Rs. 3,60,000 crore. The resources of the funds are from ongoing projects (NREGA - Rs. 2,00,000 crore, MPLAD/MLALAD - Rs. 30,000 crore and Interlinking river project - Rs. 1,00,000 crore) in addition to Rs. 60,000 crore (Rs. 30,000 crore contributed by State Government and Rs. 30,000 crore by beneficiaries) will be kept in bank as fixed deposit as sustainability funds. Fund requirement for different purposes has been worked out as follows:

• Desilting, repair and renovation of 1,80,000 km rivers and canals @ Rs. 40 lakhs per kilometer	Rs. 72,000 crore
• Desilting of 20 lakh water bodies (ponds, tanks, lakes, beals etc.) @ Rs. 5 lakhs per unit	Rs. 1,00,000 crore
• Establishment charges	Rs. 30,000 crore
• TA/DA	Rs. 20,000 crore
• Meetings, workshops, awareness programmes	Rs. 6,000 crore
• Operational/Miscellaneous expenses	Rs. 10,000 crore
• HRD (Training and Consultancy)	Rs. 12,000 crore
• Civil works, implements and goods	Rs. 50,000 crore
• Sustainability funds	Rs. 60,000 crore
Total =	Rs. 3,60,000 crore

Sharing and Resources of Funds

100 per cent project funding is by the Central Government after merging three mega projects (NREGA, MPLAD/MLALAD and Interlinking of River Projects). Three projects to be merged and renamed as National Water Security Mission.

	Heads of Expenditure	*Outlay (Rs. in crore)*
(I)	**Recurring**	
1.	Establishment	
	(a) Unskilled (manual work)	1,72,000.00
	(b) Skilled/experts/consultants	30,000.00
2.	TA/DA	20,000.00
3.	Meetings/Workshops/Awareness programmes	6,000.00
4.	Operational Expenses including hiring of vehicles/POL	10,000.00
(II)	**Human Resource Development**	
1.	Training of line department staff	6,000.00
2.	Training of water users	6,000.00
(III)	**Non-Recurring**	
1.	Civil works/repair/renovation	30,000.00
2.	Goods/Instruments	20,000.00
(IV)	**Sustainability funds**	
1.	Contribution by state government	30,000.00
2.	Contribution by beneficiaries	30,000.00
	Total	3,60,000.00

Note: Outlays under different heads are subject to review as per need.

Expenditure not to be Funded under the Project

- Expenditure on major civil works.
- Expenditure on repair/renovations not related to the project.
- Expenditure on vehicle purchase.
- Expenditure on unapproved items.
- Expenditure incurred in excess of the sanctioned budget in a financial year.

Fund Flow Mechanism

Department of Water Resources (GoI)

↓

Department of Water Resources (State Government)

↓

District (District Magistrate)

↓

Block (Block Development Officer)

↓

Village Panchayat (Village Sarpanch)

Transfer of Funds

- Electronic transfer of funds: direct, via RTG enabled Bank Branch at Block level.
- First installment as mobilization advance - 50 per cent of recurring and 100 per cent of non-recurring yearly budget.
- Six-monthly release against sanctioned budget of the financial year on receipt of physical and financial progress report.
- Revalidation of unspent funds with the approval of competent authority.

Operating the Project Account

A separate project account will be opened in a nationalized bank at block level. The account will be called National Water Security Mission and operated jointly by two nominees on behalf of the project committee.

Mode of Payment to the Workers

The workers would be paid on the basis of time and task performed by them. They have to work 9 hours including one hour of break for lunch. All the payments should be made (through bank) directly into account of wage seeker.

Annexure-A

LIST OF SCHEMES ON WATER RELATED ISSUES

Scheme	*Allocation (Rs. in crore)*	*Outcome*
Canal Irrigation Projects	Rs. 1,00,000 crore (1991-2004)	The irrigated land reduced to 146 lakh hectares (2003-04) from 178 lakh hectares (1991-92)
Accelerated Irrigation Benefit Programme (AIBP)	Launched in 1996-97 Rs. 26,000 crore spent in 15 years	Achievements are not satisfactory
National River Conservation Programme	5,000 crore Spent in last 20 years Rs. 817 crore (Ganga Action Plan) Rs. 1,306 crore (Yamuna Action Plan)	No improvement
Interlinking River Project*	Rs. 5.60 lakh crore (2002) Rs. 10 lakh crore (estimated cost at present)	The project lacks mass support due to ecological and economic reasons
Rajiv Gandhi National Drinking Water Mission	Launched in 1991 Rs. 8,000 crore (2009-10)	Targets to provide safe drinking water not fulfilled
Technology Mission to provide safe drinking water to each person	1986 (Billions of rupees spent)	Targets not achieved
Master Plan for Groundwater Recharge	Rs. 24,500 crore Prepared by Central Groundwater Board (CGWB)	Progress not satisfactory
Bharat Nirman Yojna	Rs. 1,74,000 crore (2005–09)	Target (10 Mha assured irrigation) not achieved
National Rural Employment Guarantee Scheme (NREGA)*	Rs. 40,000 crore (2010-11)	The programme lacks work plan and targets
Member of Parliament Local Area Development (MPLAD) Scheme*	Rs. 2 crore/MP/year (Rs. 1,590 crore) Likely to be raised to Rs. 5 Crore/MP/year (Rs. 4,000 crore) Also demand by MLAs (Rs.5,000 crore)	Programme has no specific work plan and faced with legal implications
Watershed Programme	Rs. 72,750 crore (2002-2022) Perspective Plan Proposed by Planning Commission	Sustainability and its impact on production is questionable

Policies/Boards/Commissions

National Water Policy	1987 (Revised in 2002)	Aim is to ensure safe drinking water to all habitations by 2012. The policy is restricted to paper only.
National Water Commission (Central Ground-water Board)	2008 (Created by Central Government)	To develop strategies for improving water conservation and water use efficiency. The progress is yet to be seen.
National River Concept	Mooted in 2006	Yet to take-off
National Ganga River Basin Authority	2009	No progress

Projects superscript with* should be merged and renamed as "NATIONAL WATER SECURITY MISSION"

INTERLINKING OF RIVERS

In spite of higher rainfall compared with other major continental areas, water is a scarce commodity in India. This is because of uneven spatial and temporal rainfall in the country. The river interlinking project was envisaged for joining rivers through reservoirs and canals to remove this natural imbalance. The plan was to divert water from water surplus area to water deficient area with an aim to alleviate flood and drought problems to enhance hydropower production and availability of water for agriculture and domestic purposes.

Genesis of Scheme

As early as 1972, the then Irrigation Minister, Mr. K.L. Rao proposed to link Ganga and Kaveri with 2640 km canal. The issue was discussed at different levels without any concrete outcome in a span of 25 years. It was again in 1999, the issue to linking rivers was raised by NDA Government. A high level task force was constituted as per Supreme Court directives in 2002 to study the feasibility of linking country's drainage systems. River Link Pact (RLP) was conceived by NDA

Government in 2003 with an aim to connect 30 rivers across India - 14 in Himalayan region and 16 in Peninsular region with targets to irrigate 37 million hectares of land, generate 34,000 million kilowatts of electricity, control floods and prevent droughts.

Post-Project Implications may prove disastrous in long-run

First MoU signed on Ken-Betwa river link between Madhya Pradesh and Uttar Pradesh Governments in August, 2005 can be used as a litmus test before taking up a grandiose project of linking India's rivers. The issues related to sharing of water (1020 mcm) and cost (Rs. 8,300 crore), relocation and resettlement of about 8,550 people and submerge of about 8,650 hectares land including 6,400 hectares of forest area were not finalized in MoU. A few contentious issues like (1) drying of Ken river to a little stream in summer may further aggravate the situation and (2) building more dams in the upstream area of Ken which may render old dams, weirs and canals redundant were also not discussed in MoU. Other distressing issues which may arise on project implementation are: (1) Ken and Betwa flow through the same part of the country with similar topography and rainfall patterns. When one is in spate, so is the other. In dry season, both have little water, (2) Betwa joins Yamuna upstream from Ken. If it carries more water, the region between the two rivers will be flooded during the monsoon while areas downstream from Ken will have droughts during rest of the year. The project, therefore, will neither mitigate floods nor droughts, rather it will aggravate the situation through the link canal, (3) Displacement of people and huge project cost are additional disadvantages of the project. (4) Even experts have not been in unison about success of the project from the very beginning. Their opinions are contradictory. Unless such contentious issues are handled, resettlement and implementation plans are carefully drawn and the affected people are consulted, the project cannot succeed. Similar is the situation with other river linking projects. Any project without evaluating its social, economic and environmental implications may prove disastrous in long-run.

Experts' Views About River Linking Project

The views of the experts who favour river linking project are: (1) to reduce incidence of floods and droughts, (2) to enhance availability of water, (3) to enhance hydro-power generation and (4) to divert water from water surplus area to water deficient area and therefore saving huge amount of river water which is flowing into the sea. The group supporting interlinking project cites examples of China and Australia where vast dry area has been converted into green belt by interlinking few important rivers.

The views of the group who do not support the project are different. Rivers have their natural course. Interlinking the rivers diverse their course which is an artificial approach and may be hazardous in long-run. With construction of dams and canals, there will be displacement of people, uprooting of trees, disturbance in ecology and perishing of aquatic life. The project will lead to destruction of cultures, communities and ecosystems of the country. It will create rifts between states and regions. The group antagonistic to interlinking rivers even support the river flooding due to many reasons. Flooding is a constructive geographical process. It creates fertile plains by depositing nutrient rich sediments, recharge the groundwater into the farmland and sustains many riparian habitats. Low frequency and high magnitude floods add new cultivable farmlands. Soviet Union is an example of adverse effects of river linking. When Swolen and Snomelt rivers of Soviet Union were interlinked with Amu and Sair rivers of Mid-Asia by 2,200 km canals, cotton production was reduced drastically. The plan to end flood problems in certain areas may not be successful because of limited lifting capacity (1,500 cubic meters) of water per second as compared to water flow per second in few rivers (normal volume of floods in the Ganga, Brahmaputra, Mahanadi and Godavari range between 30,000 and 60,000 cubic meters). During monsoon, when there is excess water in Brahmputra, the Ganga will also be in spate and even storage reservoirs will overflow, the very purpose of the project to control flood is bound to be defeated. The group even does not support the view that river linking would save huge amount of water which is flowing in the sea. Less supply of water to the oceans also have adverse effects: (1) Marine life will be deprived of nutrients supply that may adversely affect marine productivity and (2) may affect the summer monsoon in Bay of Bengal.

Other Adverse Effects of River Interlinking Project

1. Construction of a large number of huge dams and canals will have ecological and social consequences.
2. Removal of suspended sediment load from the stream flow will leave irrigation water flowing downstream of the dams nutrient depleted that ultimately affects crop production.
3. Construction of thousands of kilometers of canals in the project area will entail a loss of large tracts of land to canals and reservoirs, national parks and sanctuaries and affecting the flora and fauna of the region.
4. Huge canal networks of Punjab to augment irrigation for agriculture has proved disastrous. Overexploitation of water resources has led to waterlogging and salinity and rendered millions of hectares of good land infertile.
5. River water and its use is state subject. Several rivers are passing through more than one state. Dispute on sharing of water will further increase with linking of rivers. Dispute between Karnataka and Tamil Nadu on water sharing from Kauvery is known to everybody. Even Supreme Court's directive to Karnataka to release Kauvery water to Tamil Nadu was flouted.
6. It may also lead to dispute between countries like Bangladesh, Nepal, Bhutan and China as many rivers pass through these countries.
7. Consumption of enormous amount of electricity for pumping water will be a great drain on our energy resources.

8. The river linking project would also be against the two institutions constituted by the Government: Tiger Task Force to protect the tigers and Tribals Rights Group to recognize the rights of the tribals.

Project Cost may Shatter the Nation's Economy

The estimated project cost of Rs. 10 lakh crore may put a severe drain on government revenues and resources and shatter the nation's economy if results are not favourable. Several other projects of social and economic importance might have to be shelved or the country had to depend for such huge funds on World Bank and other agencies and as security had to mortgage rivers, like the country once mortgaged roads and bridges against borrowed money. With such staggering cost and anticipated problems, the project may ultimately be a failure.

Interlinking of rivers is not a good water management policy and alone it will not serve any purpose. Alternatively, country must concentrate to revive traditional approaches of water harvesting and conservation like watershed management, renovation, restoration and maintenance of existing tanks and reservoirs including rainwater harvesting. Finally, the interlinking river project will be the biggest human, economic and ecological disaster of Independent India. Diverting even 10 per cent of this project cost to the proposed project may bring sustainable improvement in water availability in the country.

NATIONAL RURAL EMPLOYMENT GUARANTEE SCHEME

National Rural Employment Guarantee Scheme (NREGS), an outcome of merger of two old schemes, "Food for Work Programme" and "Rural Employment Scheme", was launched in 2005 with an aim to enhance livelihood security of households in rural areas of the country by providing at least one hundred days of guaranteed employment in a year for unskilled manual work like building, repairing and desilting of ponds, small canals, check dams and contour bunds, afforestation and tree plantation, construction of rural roads and doing any other work that does not involve working with concrete. The programme was initially implemented on 2nd February, 2006 in 200 districts with budget provision of Rs. 12,700 crore. The scheme was extended to all 604 districts w.e.f. 1st April, 2008 with budget provision of Rs. 30,000 crore. Allocation has been raised to Rs. 39,000 crore for the year 2009-10. Initial wages of Rs. 60 a day have been revised to Rs. 100 a day.

Flaws in Scheme Formulation

NREGS' main focus is to provide guaranteed employment for 100 days in a year to every rural household. A worker in a family if does not get employment for 100 days in a year, he or she is entitled to unemployment allowance. The idea of making employment a right is basically wrong. Right to work, minimum livelihood security, basic education and health facilities that a country should be obliged to fulfill is O.K. But right to employment irrespective of need or no need would never be sustainable. NREGS has just become a subsidy programme. No country in the world has succeeded in providing full employment. Job creation under NREGS has diminished manpower availability for seasonal work and in places where job requirement is for targeted work. The aim should be to maximize overall job opportunities for production work in the country. Judging the performance by the number of jobs created and money spent is the main flaw in the programme. The other flaws are: (1) programme is not work oriented, (2) poor workplan and arbitrary targets, (3) lack of accountability and transparency and (4) principal responsibility for planning, implementing and monitoring at grassroots level lies with the Panchayats who do not have the competence. In other words, it is a subsidy to be provided to each rural household. How long will such subsidy continue? Full-fledged NREGS is like running a gigantic enterprise expected to have over 15 million workers. Can a country afford any such scheme? The answer is big "NO". Providing unemployment allowance if work is not decided within 15 days of registration is very funny. It is most unfortunate that a country having so many developmental agencies including Planning Commission, is incapable of identifying work and is compelled to provide unemployment allowance as the scheme is employment guarantee scheme.

Irregularities in Scheme Implementation

Numerous cases of irregularities in NREGS implementation like (1) failure in allocation of work after issuing employment letter, (2) inordinate delay in payments, (3) poor representation of women and (4) inequality in wage payments have come to limelight. Independent studies have reported several loopholes in the programme like misuse of funds, fake muster rolls, inclusion of people in the muster rolls who died and migrated, use of low quality construction material, charging people for issuing the job cards. Sometimes, even to kill people who point out irregularities in fund utilization and suicide deaths due to non-payment of wages have been noticed. Hardly 10 per cent workers get full 100 days of work or timely payment. In general, the scheme is bedeviled with corruption and administrative lapses.

Achievements and Impacts

The programme commenced on 2nd February, 2006 has now completed more than 5 years. The progress in first year was slow. 3.2 per cent of the registered households could avail 100 days of employment and the average employment was just 18 days as against the promised 100 days. First two year outcomes (2006-07 and 2007-08) of NREGS as per report card appeared in 'Hindustan Times' of February 2, 2008 are: (1) employment provided to 4.67 crore households (176 crore person days of employment), (2) Rs. 17,927 crore spent and (3) 20.66 lakh works undertaken. In the same report impacts shown are: (1) problems of poverty and unemployment in rural areas addressed, (2) durable assets created, (3) women empowerment ensured, (4) migration from rural areas reduced, (5) groundwater table raised and (6) land productivity increased. None of the outcomes and impacts are quantified and therefore have no relevance. Every project has a life and may not continue for ever. There is no sustainability plan in project formulation. Achievements are mostly physical and financial in nature and cannot be correlated with developmental process. An amount of Rs. 17,076 crore spent in year 2008-09 has been raised to Rs. 39,000 crore for the year 2009-10 and will cross Rs. 50,000 crore per year when it is implemented in full covering all the 608 districts of the country. With this kind of money there is much more that can be done for the country as a whole than is expected under this programme. One such area is to restore, renovate and revive traditional water resources of the country to avert water crisis.

MP LOCAL AREA DEVELOPMENT SCHEME

MP Local Area Development (MPLAD) scheme was started in December, 1993 with an initial allocation of Rs. 5 lakh per MP for creation of desirable assets for developmental work in their constituencies. The amount was increased to Rs. 1 crore in 1994 and Rs. 2 crore in December, 1998. There is now a proposal to increase it to Rs. 5 crore. There are 795 MPs both in Lok Sabha and Rajya Sabha in the country and if each MP is provided Rs. 5 crore as area development fund the total amount would be Rs. 3,975 crore in place of Rs 1,590 crore per year if it is Rs. 2 crore per MP. The Scheme is executed by Ministry of Statistics and Programme Implementation of Government of India. Demands for MLALAD Scheme like MPLAD Scheme have also been raised by different State Assemblies. The demand first raised in UP Assembly in 1997 was not considered because of two reasons. First, all the developmental works in the district are decided at district level in presence of MLAs. Second, the scheme involves huge amount of funds if implemented. In UP, there are 533 MLAs including MLCs which comes to Rs. 533 crore per year and Rs. 2,665 crore in a plan period of 5 years if each MLA is given Rs. 1 crore a year under the scheme. Raising such demands by other States is obvious. It will be an unending process and will not be possible for any of the State Government to meet any such demand. Total MLAs in the country are more than five thousand and if each is provided Rs. 1 crore per year, it comes more than Rs. 5000 crore per year, an amount which will shatter the total economy of the country. Secondly, every inch area of the country is covered by MPLAD funds, so allocating MLALAD Scheme would simply a duplication. In spite of that MLALAD Schemes are in place in few states. Delhi is one where each MLA gets Rs. 1 crore per year since start of the scheme in 2005-06, now raised to Rs. 2 crore per year. Such schemes have proved infectious and of no utility as per report of a study by Institute of Social Sciences.

Implementation Irregularities

Questions have been raised about implementation irregularities in MPLAD Scheme by several bodies like Institute of Social Sciences (ISS), Planning Commission and Comptroller and Auditor General (CAG) of India. Their observations are: (1) the work is not focussed, (2) overlapping of work, (3) quality of work is not satisfactory, (4) overemphasizing the scheme to serve their own interest particularly during election, (5) lack of assets creation/infrastructure development for long-term gains, (6) spending money on roads and bridges with an aim to lay foundation stones, (7) planning work without the local needs, (8) non-submission of reports in time, (9) rules are not properly followed, (10) rampant corruption, (11) lack of accountability and (12) poor control and regulation.

No Accounting System in Place

Nodal Ministry at the Center sends the money directly to the District Magistrate, who after getting the sanction from the local MP gives the money to implementing agency. After that, there is no monitoring of financial progress, *viz.*, unspent money lying with the Collectorate for years, non-submission of utilization reports in time and District Collector spends money without sanction of MP. Other financial irregularities include: poor expenditure, violation of norms in utilizing the funds, payment without verifying the work, disbursing funds without receiving utilization certificate, not maintaining the accounts properly, non-return of unused funds and releasing funds without adjusting the unspent funds of previous years, utilizing interest from unspent funds by main functionaries and misutilization of funds for the works like building of temple, mosque, church, *dharamshalas* are common practices.

Legal Flaws

The scheme is full of legal flaws. First, it contravenes the spirit of Constitution and violates decentralization process. The role of MP is to make policy which is to be implemented by executive. Second, the funds for MPLAD Scheme diverted from other on-going programmes result setback to them. Do the gains from MPLAD Scheme compensate the loss, the on-going schemes suffer? Some of the programmes wherefrom budget for MPLAD Scheme is diverted are Anganwadi, Construction of Community Centres, Primary Health Services etc. Any further increase to MPLAD Scheme would limit resources for other flagship programmes of the Government. Due to severe drought in more than 200 districts of the country in 2009, the Government allowed Members of Parliament (MPs) to utilize their local area funds to dig borewells and provide drinking water facilities. Within a week of the announcement, many drought affected areas had heavy rains and few districts resulted in floods. Such quick fix and unplanned approach does not provide any relief rather add confusion and implementation problems. The scheme also suffers from conflict of legislature and executive interests. The scheme encroaches on areas under PRIs and creates parallel power structures at the grassroots level. The development work is the job of the executive and not of the legislative body members. Legislator's role is to act as trustee of public funds by ensuring that local bodies and Government officials do not waste the State's resources. The MP with money to disburse at his own discretion under the MPLAD Scheme is against democratic approach and going back to the days of feudal system. Such schemes do not exist anywhere in the world.

Issues not in Favour of the Scheme

In the light of poor planning, implementation irregularities and legal implications, the MPLAD Scheme is confronted with several issues: (1) Is MPLAD fund benefiting those for whom it is meant? (2) Is diversion of funds from other schemes justified? (3) How do the MPs account for it? Institute of Social Sciences (ISS), National Commission for the Working of the Constitution, National Advisory Council, Administrative Reforms Committee, CAG and other bodies jointly and/or individually strongly indicted planning, implementation, monitoring and evaluation mechanism of the MPLAD scheme. All these bodies suggested for discontinuance of the scheme. Former Chief Justice of India, Justice E.S. Venkataramiah called MPLADS, "An assault to the Constitution". Scheme enabling MPs to Woo voters by using State funds is single point approach. It deforms the office of legislator and diverts him from his power duty to executive duty. As per independent review of the scheme, 60 per cent people are dissatisfied with the results and quality of work under the scheme. Should a scheme with such poor performance continue? The scheme has no production potential. There is no asset creation, no infrastructure development and almost zero outcome during a period of 16 years. Country cannot afford misuse of public money any more. Its continuance even for a day is dangerous and may jeopardize rural economy. The MPLAD fund which at present is Rs. 1590 crore per year (and may further increase 8-10 fold (15,000 crore per annum) if MPLAD fund is raised to 5 crore and MLALAD @ Rs.2 crore per MLA is introduced in Delhi) may most appropriately be utilized to address priority needs of the country. One of the top priority of the country is to address severe water crisis and the funds under MPLAD scheme be diverted accordingly.

Annexure-B

ACRONYMS

AIBP	Accelerated Irrigation Benefits Programme
BCM	Billion Cubic Meter
BIS	Bureau of Indian Standards
BNY	Bharat Nirman Yojna
BOD	Biochemical Oxygen Demand
CADP	Command Area Development Programme
CADWMP	Command Area Development and Water Management Programme
CGWA	Central Ground Water Authority
CGWB	Central Ground Water Board
CII	Confederation of Indian Industries
CPCB	Central Pollution Control Board
Cu Km	Cubic Kilometer
DDA	Delhi Development Authority
DDP	Desert Development Programme
DJB	Delhi Jal Board
DO	Dissolved Oxygen
DPAP	Drought Prone Area Programme
EIL	Engineers India Limited
GAP	Ganga Action Plan
GDP	Gross Domestic Product
GPS	Global Positioning System
Ha	Hectare
HADP	Hill Area Development Programme
ICAR	Indian Council of Agricultural Research
ICRISAT	International Crop Research Institute of Semi-Arid Tropics
IWDP	Integrated Watershed Development Programme
Km	Kilometer
LCPD	Liters per Capita per Day
MCD	Municipal Corporation of Delhi
MCM	Million Cubic Meter
MGD	Million Gallon per Day

M ha	Million Hectare
MLD	Million Liter per Day
MM	Millimeter
MoU	Memorandum of Understanding
MPLADS	Member of Parliament Local Area Development Scheme
MSqKm	Million Square Kilometer
NAP	National Afforestation Programme
NASA	National Aeronautics and Space Authority
NCMP	National Common Minimum Programme
NDA	National Democratic Alliance
NGO	Non-Governmental Organization
NGRBA	National Ganga River Basin Authority
NRCP	National River Conservation Programme
NREGS	National Rural Employment Guarantee Scheme
NWC	National Water Commission
NWDPRA	National Watershed Development Project for Rainfed Areas
NWHN	National Water Harvesters' Network
NWC	National Water Commission
NWRC	National Water Resources Council
PPB	Parts Per Billion
RGNDWM	Rajiv Gandhi National Drinking Water Mission
RLP	River Link Project
RTI	Right to Information
RVP & FPR	River Valley Projects and Flood Prone Rivers
SHGs	Self-Help Groups
SqKm	Square Kilometers
SSP	Sardar Sarovar Project
STP	Sewage Treatment Plant
TDS	Total Dissolved Salts
UN	United Nations
VIP	Very Important Person
WALMI	Water and Land Management Institute
WDPSCA	Watershed Development Project in Shifting Cultivation Areas
WHO	World Health Organization

WUAs	Water User Associations
WWD	World Water Day
WWF	World Wide Fund
YAP	Yamuna Action Plan

Index